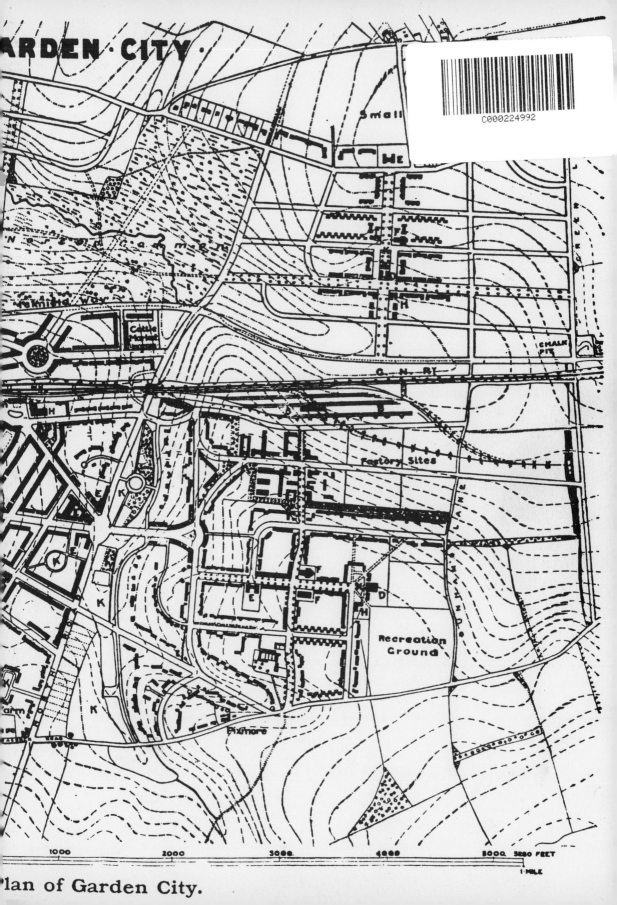

Plan of Garden City.

LETCHWORTH
RECOLLECTIONS

LETCHWORTH RECOLLECTIONS

A unique record of life in The First Garden City
as remembered by some of its earliest citizens
1903 - 1939

*Co-ordinated by Heather Elliott
and John Sanderson*

Edited by Maureen Maddren

EGON PUBLISHERS LTD

Front endpaper: *Plan of the Garden City as printed in an early guide to the Garden City.*

Half title: *Members of The First Garden City Band c1908.*

Title spread: *The corner of Leys Avenue and Eastcheap in the early 1930s.*

Page 5: *A photograph from a 1912 advertising campaign for Spirella corsets.*

Back endpapers: *A map of Letchworth Garden City in the 1990s.*

Copyright © Egon Publishers Ltd 1995

ISBN 0 905858 96 4

Designed by Nick Maddren
Campion Publishing Services, Baldock SG7 6DB
for Egon Publishers Ltd

Printed in England by
Streets Printers, Royston Road, Baldock, Herts SG7 6NW

Contents

Acknowledgements

We should like to acknowledge the co-operation given to us by the following, without whom this book would not have been possible.

Interviewers and Transcribers
Pat Carr, Sheila Carrick, Suzanne Dorkacz, Heather Elliott, Mark Elliott, Joyce Elson, John Elson, Ian Frearson, Terry Friend, Julie Goodwyn, Rodney Hall, Liz Hamilton, Owen Hardisty, Edna Imber, Elizabeth Jackson, Mel Knights, Vera Morley, Samantha Roberts, Gordon Rogers, Brenda Rogers, John Sanderson, Daphne Sutcliffe, Joan Walker, Enid Willey.

We should also like to thank the following people who either agreed to be interviewed, provided written recollections, loaned photographs or helped in some other way.

Mrs Doris Allsop, Miss Ethel Andrews, Mrs Arlick, Miss Austin, Mr Baker, Mrs Barbara Barry-Parker, Mr John Basford, Mrs Gertrude Basham, Joan and Ralph Berrett, Mrs Elsie Betts, L Bichener, Mrs Vera Bilson, Mrs Monica Bird, Mr and Mrs G Blows, Mr George Bollen, Mr Colin Bywaters, Miss D. Cade, Jim and Doreen Cadwallader, Mr Bill Carr, Jim Cave, Mrs Vera Cheesman, Winifred Collins, Mr and Mrs A Collins, Mr and Mrs J Collins, Mrs Lucy Cooper, Miss Maureen Corry, Mr George Cotton, Monica Cracknell, John Cruse, Fred Cutts, Mrs Freda Diss, Mr R J Duncombe, Mrs Frances Dunn, Mrs Joan Edwards, Ella Edwards, Mrs Joan Everett, Mrs Garratt, Mr Sidney Gentle, Mr Jack Gifford, Sidney Gravett, Mrs Phyllis Green, Mr and Mrs Donald Griggs, Mrs Hacker, Mrs Sheila Hardy, Miss Marion Hargraves, Mrs Lenora Hawkins, Mr Claude Ingrey, Mr Glyn Jones, David King, Mr James Lee, Bertha Leech, Marjory Lynch, Mr Maine, Miss Edna Mallett, Mr P J Miles, Mrs Pegeen Mole, May Morgan, Mr James Morley, Telford Morton, Alec and Vi Norris, Miss Dorothy Odell, Margaret Payne, Eric and Alice Plum, Margaret Pooley, Ida Price, Mrs P Price, Freda Pullen, Desmond Rix, Miss Billie Rogers, Miss Ena Rogers, Mrs Vera Roth, Richard Sale, Mr Satchell, Mr Jack Seaton, Mr James Seaton, Margaret Sherbourne, Mrs Louise Sparkes, Frank Spary, Esther Speed, Peter Speltinckx, Mrs Irene Stacey, Mr Harold Stokes, Mrs Nancy Stone, Mrs Winnie Stubbs, Mr Edward Sumsion, Mr Hubert Tanner, Jeff and Connie Thacker, Christabel Thomas, Miss Elaine Tickle, Mr Walter Titmus, Mr Stanley Tomkins, Mrs W Tomkins, Mrs L Vallance, Mrs Varley, Mrs Joan Varley, Mrs Elizabeth Vickery, Mr Charles E Walker, Mrs Joan Walker, David Warburton, W Ward, Mrs Win Warner, Miss Winifred Watson, Mrs Betty Wearmouth, Mrs Joyce Wharton, Mrs Brenda Wightman, Mr Roy Woodward.

We acknowledge, too, the help and support of Letchworth Garden City Corporation, Letchworth Arts and Leisure Group, and the staff of Letchworth Heritage Museum.

Whilst every effort has been made to credit the owners of all the illustrations and the originators of some of the information used in this book, we regret any omission that may have occured.

Bibliography
Johnson, Kenneth, *The Book of Letchworth* (Barracuda, 1975)
Lancaster, Robert, *Letchworth Garden City in Camera* (Quotes Ltd, 1986)
Lancaster, Robert, *Letchworth Garden City in Old Picture Postcards* (European Library, 1994)
Miller, Mervyn, *Letchworth, The First Garden City* (Phillimore, 1989)

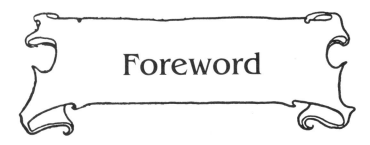

Foreword

When we started on the *Letchworth Recollections* project early in 1994, I don't think we realised how many people had stories to tell or how much enthusiasm there was for such a project.

Letchworth Recollections came about as a result of discussions between John Street, who has published similar local history books, and William Armitage, who was an instigator of the Letchworth Arts and Leisure Group. One of the roles of the LALG is to assist groups of people, who are interested in a common topic, to get together. So it was that early in 1994, a meeting was set up to bring together people who were interested in the early days of Letchworth. Many of those who came to the first meeting had stories to tell, but others such as ourselves, were interested to hear those stories or to help with compiling and capturing the information.

We established a core group of 'information collectors' and began to work down our list of 'information providers'. We wanted to make sure that all those people who had stories to tell about Letchworth knew of our project, so we had stalls at the local Ideas Fair and Fun Day. This worked and our list grew and grew. Most of the people who wanted to tell us their stories were in Letchworth and surroundings but we had one contributor from York and were even contacted from America about a potential interviewee. In the end we had over 200 names of people who potentially had stories to tell.

Once the list of interviewees was compiled the *Letchworth Recollections* group set about recording interviews with those who wanted to tell their story. In the end we captured the stories of over 100 people. In addition, they provided us with nearly 200 photographs of those early days.

We have found that the collection of the information has been fascinating. We have learnt that the logistics of tracking all the names, tapes, transcriptions, photos etc needs quite a bit of planning. We have found that people's memory of places and place names is different. Mostly though, we have caught a glimpse of life as it was in the early days of Letchworth, a town with new ideals, the first garden city.

That is what this book is about. We hope you enjoy it.

Heather Elliott   John Sanderson

Introduction

Ebenezer Howard had a dream – to build a garden city where people could live and bring up children in a clean, healthy environment surrounded by trees and green spaces. He lived to see that dream made reality and this book is an attempt to record the feel of the early days of Letchworth Garden City and its gradual growth up to the outbreak of the Second World War.

It is not a history book. The factual details of how the First Garden City came into being are well recorded in the numerous books about the town already produced. In *Letchworth Recollections*, the citizens speak for themselves. This is how they remembered their childhood, first jobs, leisure time, the shops and the many characters who were attracted to this new vibrant concept in semi-urban living.

Running a clothes stall at a bazaar in the Mrs Howard Memorial Hall c1908.

Those who do not know Letchworth well may be surprised at how advanced the town seems to have been. Many free thinkers were drawn here – there were animal rights activists, political activists, conscientious objectors, philosophers, artists, writers, craftsmen and women and, of course, vegetarians.

Some readers, who know the town and its history well, may consider there have been some surprising omissions, but, as already stated, this was never intended to be a complete record of precisely how the town grew, which roads, shops, businesses and so on came to the town and when. People's memories, too, are selective and each person remembers what was important to him or her. We have chosen anecdotes that we hope cover a wide range of subjects, some touching, many humorous, but all, we believe, will add something to the knowledge of this unique place – there have been other garden cities, but this was the first! We have also tried, as far as possible, or practicable, to put events in chronological order within each section.

Over 100 tapes were made, so the task of editing this book was not easy – there was much material to choose from. We hope something from every tape has been used. Where memories were similar, two or three may have been combined to produce a fuller account of an occasion or event. So if you don't recognise your actual words, be assured that whatever you told us has been of enormous help.

It goes without saying that this book would not have been possible without the generous co-operation of all the people who either agreed to be interviewed or wrote down their memories for us. Thanks are also due to the interviewers and transcribers, all of whom are named elsewhere in this book, who, often through dedicated perseverance, produced some remarkable interviews and faithful transcriptions.

As well as producing *Letchworth Recollections*, the other aim of this project was to provide, in the form of the tapes and transcriptions, a valuable resource, which could be used in the future for research purposes and particularly for school projects, so that children growing up in Letchworth would learn, from an early age, the importance of the town they live in through listening to or reading the actual words of some of its earliest citizens.

The whole project would not have come about without the remarkable organisational abilities of Heather Elliott and John Sanderson who sought out interviewees and paired them with a band of interviewers, most of whom had never tackled the daunting task of interviewing before. And then kept track of tapes, recorders, transcriptions and, most importantly, photographs, in a military-like fashion.

Thanks are also due to Bob Lancaster, Curator of the Heritage Museum, for generously giving time to go through his vast collection of photographs and provide us with additional illustrative material for the book.

Finally, I should like to thank Chris Maddren and Tim Maddren, who, particularly in the latter stages of the book, put in countless hours to help ensure that we made the deadline.

Maureen Maddren

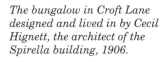

The bungalow in Croft Lane designed and lived in by Cecil Hignett, the architect of the Spirella building, 1906.

The Old Post Office, Letchworth.

Norton. Garden City. Church Yard.

1
A fresh start

At the turn of the century change was in the air – advances were being made in science and technology and transport. The spirit of optimism that pervaded Edwardian England produced just the right climate for many to feel excited at the prospect of uprooting to take part in the birth of a totally new concept in living – a garden city. People from all over the country were attracted to the idea – for some it was an escape from the grime of the city, while others saw job prospects here.

I'm now 93 and I've lived in Letchworth on and off for about 85 years. My parents came from Rugby and my father joined the Letchworth Company as works superintendent for the First Garden City. In those days there was no urban district council. The First Garden City Company was all-powerful. You had to get their permission for anything you wanted to do, even paint your house, you had to get permission to have the colour you wanted.

My father's uncle, John Openshaw, came to Letchworth in 1903. He was a builder down from Lancashire to start a company here with the idea that the Garden City was an ideal way of

Far top left: *Letchworth Corner sub-post office, in Hitchin Road photographed c1910. A carefully posed picture with three children on the left standing decorously around the bench and the postman with his delivery bicycle on the right.*

Far bottom left: *Early Edwardian photograph of Norton taken from the churchyard of Norton Church.*

Left: *A double-fronted bungalow in Rushby Mead, built by John Openshaw, who came to Letchworth from Lancashire in 1903. This bungalow was priced at £300.*

·BUNGALOW·IN·RUSHBY·MEAD·LETCHWORTH·   BUILT BY J·T·OPENSHAW & Cº PRICE £300

Ebenezer Howard, founder of the First Garden City at Letchworth, 1903.

conducting life. He was a very idealistic sort of man and very keen to be a pioneer in the new venture. He was on the first Parish Council in 1907 and after the First World War he invited my father and his first cousin to join his building company. My Grandfather (G. Bennett) came to live in Letchworth when he retired after the First World War.

I was the sixth and youngest daughter in our family and my father was one of the very early builders in Letchworth.

At the turn of the century my mother and father came back from several years in South Africa. On arrival in London, my parents rented a house in Clapham whilst my father looked around for a place for them to settle. The new and promising development in Letchworth Garden City appealed to him and he and my mother came down by train to view the possibilities. My mother later told me how surprised they were on climbing the many steps from the platform to the ticket office to find themselves viewing a stretch of country almost devoid of houses.

My father, C. F. Townsend, knew Ebenezer Howard and that's why he came to Letchworth and camped here in 1903, but he actually brought his family here permanently in 1905. First of all they lived in a wooden house in Wilbury Road, I think it was a bungalow actually – and three years later he moved into a house that he had built in Norton Road, no. 66.

My grandfather Richard Thacker was assistant station master at Wood Green and came to Letchworth in 1904. Father walked up from Hitchin up the track until he came to the old Letchworth station, which was then on the far side of the bridge from where it is now. He located where he was going to work, and went off to find somewhere to lodge; he finally walked to Baldock where he found my other grandfather and his wife living, and agreed lodgings with them. And that was how the two families first became known. My other grandfather was Ben Parker who came to Letchworth, I'm not quite sure when he came, but he originally worked for a firm in Works Road, who were making mastic roofing, and then he set up in business as a contractor at Norton Hall Farm and became a contractor over quite a wide area, he did a lot of work in Letchworth, a lot of the laying of drains and so on and at some point in time bought the first four houses, the first four odd numbered houses in Glebe Road. And both families, the Thackers and Parkers moved into them together with the family of the Seatons, who were quite well known in Letchworth and still are, and some people called King.

I was born in the village of Henlow on June 21, 1904. At that time my father worked for the local butcher, part of his time in the shop and part of his time looking after their various flocks of poultry. In 1907 he wanted a better job and so applied for one at Hatfield. The people there applied to his present employers for a reference and because he had applied for another job his employers dismissed him. There was no other work in the village but he had heard there were jobs going in Letchworth so he applied to the firm of Davies and Ball for a job which he was given. He was taken on as a general labourer which meant putting in many of the gas and water and sewerage services in the town, as well as helping on various other jobs on the roads and so on. They decided, Mum and Dad, to move to Letchworth in 1908, I was then just over three.

My parents came to Letchworth in 1906. I was born here in 1915. They had met Ebenezer Howard in London. He used to lecture at the Congregational Church which they attended and they were so fired with his ideals and his plans for the Garden City that they decided they would like to move here. So my mother cycled down from London to look around, to see if they could find anywhere to live because my father worked in London and would have to travel each day. She rented a cottage in Ridge Road which was only about four feet high at the time, but they knew it would be finished by the time they were married. And that's how they came to Letchworth.

We lived there for just about two years, but they liked the Garden City so much they decided to stay and they had this

One of the reasons people came to the Garden City was because of the spacious nature of the town. This house in Ridge Road had, like many others, a large garden.

Letchworth Lane, c1910.

SOUTH FRONT

house, where I'm living now, designed by Clapham Lander, an architect. It was built by John Ray who was one of the main builders in Letchworth at that time, and they moved into this house in 1908, just before my eldest brother was born.

Our maternal grandfather, John Frederick Bennett, bought no.4 Cross Street (one of the cheap 1905 cottage exhibition buildings) and moved to Letchworth in 1907. He suffered from asthma and it was his 17th move since his marriage. Letchworth proved to be the only place where he could live with his condition. Coming from London, the horse-drawn van was too tall to get under the cattle creep, which was the only way to get across the railway line and he had to go all the way round Baldock to get to Cross Street – still the only 'Street' in Letchworth.

He was also very musical and played the cello in the early Letchworth Orchestra and we have been told that in the very early days he sometimes used to take an 'His Master's Voice' gramophone, which we can remember, up to The Sheds to entertain the workers in the evening.

Our paternal grandfather, William Rogers, came to Letchworth about 1909-1910. He lived in Station Road and opened a shoe and repair shop there and later, when Leys Avenue was completed, a second one next to the Midland Bank. My father worked with him, both on sales and repairs. We had a long back garden with a path leading to where the repairs were carried out.

My grandmother read about Letchworth and moved the family from Wolverhampton to a house on the corner of Lytton Avenue and Pixmore Way in 1912. She was very interested in the Garden

The post office, c1913, stands in splendid isolation in the Broadway. The building under construction in the background is the railway station.

City idea. My father came from Towcester after the 1914-18 war – he worked at Phoenix cars and later Marmet.

My father arrived here in 1910. He walked from Hounslow in Middlesex and got a job as a dustman. We lived in Icknield Way in a small wooden bungalow facing the common, that was very dense then. I think it belonged to the Howard Cottage Society. Then we went to Boscombe Place and my mother lived here right until she died at the age of 89.

I have lived in Letchworth for 80 years and my parents came to Letchworth for work and they were some of the first people to work in Letchworth – they had to live in Baldock before the houses were built here and they used to have to bring their water up for making tea. My father worked for the Permanite Company – they did mastic roofing.

My mother's people escaped from Belgium when war broke out because the Germans were coming into Antwerp. We came to England on Christmas Day 1914. We had a boat then you see, and they landed us in England at Harwich. And they put us into what I thought was a college, a girls' college, but I found out later on that it was the workhouse. But it looked like a college to me. It was a lovely big, nice building you know, in Streatham. We then went to live with relations in Woolwich, but in 1915, when I was about 17, my father began to have trouble with his stomach and the doctor said that the London air didn't suit him – he should go and live in the country. Well, as it happened, my youngest sister lived in Letchworth already – they moved from London to Letchworth, because Kryn and Lahy was there, along with the

Right: *Painting of Eastholm Green by Frank Dean.*

Below: *Station Road, c1910, before the main post office in the Broadway was built. At the end of the road is the, then, head post office.*

French and Belgian people and that's how we came to be in Letchworth. We lived in Burnell Rise.

When I came out of that station, I thought, 'Oh, what a place to come to, I'm being buried alive here.' There was nothing here. We stood there, and on that side was all fields. There was no Brooker's, there was no big buildings, there was one opposite – it was a men's outfitters shop. I remember that. And next door was a small shop, that was a little tea shop. You could go and get a cup of tea and cake in there. But that was all there was. All there is now on the Broadway wasn't there. And Eastcheap, the last house in Eastcheap was what they used to call the colonnade, at that corner, you know the colonnade, that was a lovely crockery shop there, and then there was our pork butcher – our pork butcher, we used to call him.

The attractions were many for my family being Quakers, vegetarian and forward thinking on many fronts. Charlie who was a qualified architect and surveyor, obtaining a position in the office of Barry Parker and Raymond Unwin.

My father was in the Belgian army and got wounded during the early days of World War I; he convalesced in Shropshire. Having worked for one of the Kryn and Lahy factories he was asked to come and work in Letchworth in 1915.

My father worked at Moss's in the warehouse – lived in Hitchin – moved to Letchworth when the houses in The Quadrant were built. They started to build them in 1915 and we were the first people in those houses. You would have to bike from Hitchin because there were no buses in those days. So it was for convenience that they moved. This would have been about 1918.

We came to Letchworth in 1915 mainly because my father worked in Letchworth and at the time he was told if you work in Letchworth you ought to come and live in Letchworth. As he worked at the Spirella – that was in 1910 – we had first choice of Howard Cottage houses – because there was an agreement between Kincaid and Ebenezer Howard – mainly because Kincaid, who was the American boss of Spirella, wanted all the ground around the Spirella to build houses on for his workers.

So we came to live in Campers Road and in those days – 1920s – nearly all Campers Road and Campers Walk were Spirella employees. Of course, as they progressed with more money they bought houses or, later on, the firm bought the houses and let them have them at a low mortgage. My mother's father was a horse trader and they bought horses locally and sold them to the other branch of the family in London to sell to the gentry, because there was no such thing as motor cars.

My parents came from Leeds to Letchworth in 1919 for my father to get work. He found work at Dent's publishers and printers, then called Temple Press. They lived originally in Pix Road, in rooms, then they got rooms in Barton Hill, two rooms upstairs, and the landlady kindly allowed me to be born there. We thought that was rather good of her. When I was 14 months old we moved to Temple Gardens. That was owned by Dent's. That's why it was called Temple Gardens. A lot of the neighbours were employees of Dent's. It was quite a big house. It was quite nice as well.

My family used to be farmers – bridging one farm at Stotfold and another one at Charlton – we also had a small farm, Wilbury Farm down Wilbury Road which is opposite Standalone Farm, but we moved to Standalone Farm in 1919, it being previously occupied by the Belgian Refugees during the 14 – 18 War.

Well, we came from Dublin in the early 1920s. My father was a policeman in the Royal Irish Constabulary. And of course they

were disbanded, and they went over to home rule in southern Ireland. So, we had the choice of coming to Letchworth or old Woking, and my father along with many other police families came to Letchworth. We settled in Jackman's Place, where the houses were just being completed, and for my parents it must have been a big upheaval, coming from a city. Anyway, some of the police found security jobs, and others managed on their police pensions.

My father came here from Markyate to work on the railways – he was a porter, and my husband's father came from London having worked at the ABC restaurant as a cook. He came here as a cook for the road makers, that was in 1905, I think, and then consequently he liked the town, what he saw of it, and he stayed there, stayed on not as a cook but in various other jobs. Then he brought his family down and they moved from various places and eventually settled in Pix Road where my husband was born in 1907.

You had lots of things to do in Letchworth. I think it was a beautiful place anyway. So did my mother, when she got used to it. She cried every day, I think, for two years when she came up from London. She used to work in a bank in London, you see, then come down to here. She thought it was terrible, well really she liked it, but missed her mum and her sisters. But Mr Hardy, that was Meredew's boss, he moved all his workforce down from London – they all came, no one turned it down.

When we first came to Letchworth we lived in Wilbury Road and the garden backed onto fields as they were then, they are all houses now. It was all fields before you came to the common. I can remember sitting up in a big conker tree which we had at the bottom of the garden and watching two big traction engines pulling a plough backwards and forwards across the fields. I think they were Fowler engines, but I'm not sure.

My parents came to Letchworth in 1931. My father worked for a clearing house in London, and he heard that there were houses in Letchworth, council houses, vacant – if you can believe that in this day and age, and they decided to come to Letchworth because it was a pleasant town. I think the rents were slightly cheaper than they were in North London, even in those days there was the differential between the areas, and we moved to Letchworth in October '31.

My father heard of Letchworth through Charlie Sax, who also worked at the clearing house you see. I think he was responsible for a lot of emigrants to Letchworth in those days, and it was a very pleasant town, you know, green countryside as opposed to the streets of London.

We came to Letchworth in 1934 when I was 10. Dad was in Customs and Excise and he came to work as the Customs Officer at the Anglia Match Company. Now you might think, why do you need a Customs Officer at the Anglia Match Company? Apparently the production of matches, probably still the same today, comes under the Explosives Act, so therefore all the matches produced were subject to duty and it was Dad's job to see that all the matches, when they were produced, were put into bonded store until the duty was paid.

I came to Letchworth in 1934 but I had heard of it a good ten years before that because I lived just outside Nottingham, where I went to school, and on the train – the old Great Northern – in the carriages there were advertisements for Letchworth Garden City on the Hitchin to Cambridge branch line with pictures of houses and some of the factories.

2
Early Days

So, having attracted workers from all over the country as well as those living in nearby towns and villages, the First Garden City had to house and feed them. There were few shops, so a growing army of tradesmen would come round delivering foodstuffs and household essentials directly to the door. Those who were children at the time recalled them vividly.

It could well be how it all started in 1899 when my grandparents came to live in Icknield Way under a row of beech trees where it joins Green Lane. There were no cottages, absolutely nothing. They came here in 1899 from Tewin into a wooden bungalow. It was provided by the Arlesey Brickworks and Grandfather worked the chalk pit with a gang of men, the chalk pit that runs a little bit further down the line, just a stone's throw from the bridge. Of course, the railway was there so I imagine that it was carted away along the railway.

When they came from Tewin, the only way in, so I've heard it said, was to come along Baldock Road, for some reason they couldn't get down Dunhams Lane, it was probably just a track then. And they had to go along the Baldock Road, down into Baldock and up the original Icknield Way to the bottom of Green Lane. They lived there for probably four years – well until the houses became available in Green Lane and then they moved up there. Their bungalow was parallel to the railway line with the garden backing on to it. They had no water or anything. I've heard it said that the engine drivers would pull up and give them water from the trains and I suppose they had paraffin. They had no sanitation either. Their nearest neighbours were Baldock, Norton, Standalone, Willian and there was a farmhouse where Letchworth Hospital is now.

They went to school up Green Lane to Norton, again I've heard it said that they chased pheasants down the cart track in Green Lane, which in those days wouldn't have been a made up road – it would have been a green lane. And there were sheep. There was a spring half way down Green Lane where the water was retrieved for cattle. There was a brickyard at the top where the shops are by Norton Corner, and just as you go round into Norton there was a green there as you turn into Croft Lane much larger than it is now, and sheep were dipped there.

Before the First World War, the shops in Letchworth only went up as far as is now The Arcade. The Arcade wasn't there and then there were the shops down Leys Avenue and just two or three in Eastcheap. There were many private shops. There were at least four or five grocers in those days. There was Snare's at the bottom of Station Road, there was Goodman's at the corner of The Wynd (which is now the betting shop) there was the Star Tea Company down Leys Avenue, there was a Home & Colonial Stores (which is now where the Nationwide Building Society is) and there was another one. The Co-op had their place first of all in Leys Avenue (over what is now the DER building) and then they transferred to their premises in Eastcheap, so there was that number of grocers. There were also four or five butchers, nowadays we only have one private butcher. There was two in Eastcheap beside the Co-op, there was Broughton's, the pork butcher, and Ansell's on the other side of the road, there was a London Central Meat Company and at least one other, I can't remember the name of that one.

The clothing stores – there was at least five men's clothing stores. There was Rawlinson's on one side of the road, Butler's on the other, Pugh's in Station Place, the Co-op, and Spink's, of course, the men's on one side and the ladies' drapers on the other.

There were two or three families and they lived in a house round the corner from Lytton Avenue in Pixmore Way. The men had long hair and long beards and wore smocks and sandals. Women had long straight hair. Boys and girls used to tease them and run around them and call them Jesus. Eventually they were tired of living in the house and went to live in caravans. I understand they had a caravan and tents for a short while at Norton, then they left Letchworth in the early part of the First World War.

There weren't many buses in the early days and nobody had got cars or anything, so we'd go shopping to Hitchin by train –

4-ft. Fumed Oak
Dresser Sideboard,

tuppence ha'penny return. It was a good walk from Letchworth Station, up to Green Lane but nothing was built up, it was just fields, so you could cut across. We used to cut across the green and then we used to go over the railway sidings, you know, go over the railway itself, where the trains run, down the other bank, go over and into the top end of Birds Hill, that's what we used to do. There was no factories or nothing, it was all open, and all the way along the only thing I can remember of the factories coming was Enfield and the motorbikes, they had the first factory here, a long way before British Tabulated. I remember British Tabulated, going up brick by brick. That was all open fields you see.

After the war building continued – it was still quite rural though. Jackman's Place was built after the First World War and the houses that are at the side of Pixmore Avenue and Pixmore Way were built, because when we first went to school to Pixmore from higher up Pixmore Way, that ended at Norton Way South and

Aerial view of the Spirella factory nearing completion 1920. There are still many roads almost devoid of buildings, with very little along the Broadway and many paths still criss-crossing the town.

there was a footpath and footbridge over the Pix. And then we used to cross a field that came out at Shott Lane and go along Shott Lane and there was a little path up to one of the school gates.

We did that in the summer, but of course you couldn't go across the field in the winter. Then we had to go down and up Hillshott and along Ridge Avenue and up Broughton Hill to School Walk.

My father became Secretary of what was then called the Share Purchase Society. A number of people wanted to own shares in the Garden City Company and I assume they hadn't got a great deal of money so he used to spend every Saturday afternoon collecting shillings from the people who wanted to buy shares and when they had enough money to buy one share they would draw lots and whoever won got the first share. And they continued to do that, drawing lots in rotation so that they all got a share, before they started on the next one. My father actually worked in London – he was a Civil Servant and he used to go up and down each day.

View down Station Road, with a complete row of shops of many different architectural designs on the right. Howard Cottages are on the left of the picture.

When they first built this area – the Westbury area – it finished at High Avenue. Then in the 20s they built Hillbrow and Chiltern View on top of it. I remember the then Duke of York coming and

Station Road, Letchworth Garden City

77908.

standing in the road and all the kids waving their flags and cheering as they went by.

When we came to Campers Road they were just getting the foundations out for the Council houses so it was a bit muddy. Of course, tarmac roads were unknown.

I remember the springs. Where those two bungalows are in Spring Road they are built on the springs. When they first dug those foundations out, they'd go to lunch and when they came back the trenches had filled with water so they had to put them on pylons – they didn't realise – because you appreciate you can't tell people coming into the town what is here. And there were some sand and gravel pits around here behind the Marmet – where these new houses are built.

From the top of Icknield Way where Simmond's Coach Garage is right down to Chater-Lea, that used to be one great big field, there were no factories at all. They used to have fairs and a circus on that field. I can remember the only factory in Icknield Way was the old mineral water factory, who used to make Idris mineral water. This area here, Icknield Green, I remember when they were building the houses on the Wilbury Estate, this was a great big lake. I don't know why it was a lake, I suppose it could

Garden City Small Holdings Ltd, 1908. This was in Archway Road which ran from Nevells Road by the side of the Skittles Inn to Norton Way North. The road was closed when the railway bridge in Norton Way North opened.

Below: *Howard Hall, 1909, built in memory of Mrs Ebenezer Howard.*

Right: *View across Nevells Road and Norton Way North c1909.*

have been the water draining from where they were building the houses. With all the wood everywhere we used to make rafts and row about all round here. I remember it all before Bedford Road, Cowslip Hill, none of them were there. My father used to have a strawberry field in Wilbury Road. We grew the strawberries and he would buy the whole field up and sell them. There was nothing here at all. In fact there was a time when you knew practically everybody in Letchworth.

Now my father, he got married in about 1922/24 and I was born in 1926 in Hitchin and they moved into a house in Spring Road down the cul-de-sac – now that's my first impressions of Letchworth. They then moved further down Spring Road nearer the bridge, and it was here that the houses used to have ranges, gas lighting, coal cellars but also they had wonderful fields at the back where we used to have gangs and play underneath the oak tree and build tents and play cowboys and Indians. It's also at this time that the milkman used to come round with a cart and a big churn and mother used to go out with a milk jug and you used to measure it into a half pint or pint metal pot and pour it into her jug. Also, even in those days, we were warned about tramps and not to go near them when they came down the road begging. Letchworth was a wonderful place for children because there was all the woods along by the railway and they used to be wonderful for climbing and watching the trains go past and waving to the engine drivers.

Garden City North.

As a child here I remember the street traders who would come round making their rounds regularly. I helped the milkman when I was younger, but when I was about 11 I worked at the Triangle after school. This was the Triangle Stores in Common View. A crumpet man used to come round on Sunday. There was Mrs Cooper, who lived in Common View, she used to make wonderful faggots. They used to call her 'Faggot Cooper'. There were the butchers, Hopper, Smith and Barnes, used to come round to the door. Corn Merchants, Clark, Longley and Guest. Nott's, Co-op and Redrup who were Letchworth Bakers; Farr, Barker, Juff and Hanscombe were from Baldock. Nottage came from Stotfold – that was a mother and daughter who used to come round with their horse-drawn cart, and Osborne came from Walsworth.

Then there were the greengrocers, Green and Dellar from Ashwell who used to have a mule to pull his cart; then there was Bygrave from Baldock and Sabey who used to live in Green Lane.

The Luton hatters used to come round two or three times a year, generally in the evening, I expect, when people would be at home, to sell ladies' hats. Then there was Hartley's hardware, Spencer and Westall. Then there were coalmen, Ellis and Everard, Franklin, Pearson, Pearry, Berry, Sadler and Jermyn. Then there were shoe-repairers. This Sid Cooper used to have a shed at the back of the house, and we used to watch him shoe mending.

A tennis party in early Letchworth where clubs and societies proliferated and where it was an ideal place to grow up.

The road in Common View wasn't made up when I can remember. I remember Ben Parker because he had one of these traction engines and he did the roads. The sweet shops in Common View were Maynard, Bourne, Nichols – these weren't shops, they were all from the houses. But when the Triangle Stores opened then the Council made them finish. Then there were the milkmen, Squires, Central Dairies, Parrish from Willian, Dancock from Glebe Road and Bygrave – he lived in Croft Lane – they had a farm. Then there were the beer merchants. There was Carter from Wilbury Hills Road. He used to come round with Fremlin's Ales. Then Foreman's from Ashwell and Flitton's from Stotfold and Gulliver's from Baldock. Albert Calcraft used to come round with the evening newspaper – about half-past five at night. Later they had a fish stall outside Smiths.

We used to get the old organ-grinders round the street, singers, men with spoons – it's known as spoon-bashing where they have a couple of spoons and make a tune out of them.

I lived in Nevells Road then, and used to walk across the railway along what is now the Broadway between fields of waving corn. And there was a path, just an ordinary footpath right in the middle where the actual track of the road itself is now, and a couple of rows of trees which they'd planted on either side which of course now are very mature. The Broadway must have been

Mr Westall, manager of the Garden City Co-operators with his bread delivery van.

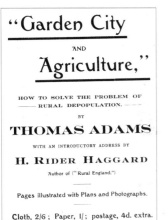

Right: The 1904 plan of Letchworth, designed by Barry Parker and Raymond Unwin, architects of the new Garden City.

finished off in the 20s I should say, because there was quite a number of fair sized houses along there then. But the town square was only half done. It was completed as far as where the Post Office and Council Office is now.

I happened to be born in Hitchin, which is an old town mentioned in the Domesday Book, and although I don't remember this, I was told that Hitchin people were quite horrified at the thought of this new town being built on their doorstep. After the First World War I used to be brought up by my nurse on an open topped double-decker bus to see this extraordinary town of Letchworth. The idea of seeing Letchworth from my nurse's point of view was to see the sights of the people, long-haired men, men in togas, sandals, on curious little bicycles and in fact so very un-Hitchin like that it really became an open topic of conversation.

The old Broadway originally was a road from the Hitchin Road to what is now called the Sollershot Circus. From then on it became a cinder path going down approximately as far as where the old council office now stands. At that point there was a white bandstand that held regular brass band concerts. At the end of the twenties this cinder path was widened into a macadam road; it had been originally intended to be a straight main road to the station but the station was built a few yards to the west so the Broadway lost its straight line to the entrance. At Sollershot Circus six roads enter around a circle, Spring Road north and south, Sollershot east and west and the Broadway north and south. My father-in-law Barry Parker, realising that a six road junction would cause problems, designed a roundabout, reputed to be the first in the world but certainly the first in the British Isles, an interesting invention for a man who had never driven a car.

I think that the great attraction of Letchworth in those early days was because it was a new idea; something without any past history, built between two old towns of Hitchin and Baldock and the two villages Willian and Norton. The people who came to live here were in a new century, artists, craftsmen, writers and scholars and of course many manufacturers making new products and again with new ideas for the future of this century. Possibly its greatest enemy is the motor car. The early pioneers at the last years of the 19th century could not conceive that such a revolution over the horse-drawn vehicle and bicycles could possibly happen. Our residential roads are far too narrow for parking and moving traffic, and the majority of houses have no room for garages and parking space.

Letchworth will be forever remembered as the First Garden City, what a pity we did not keep our name in full and set the pattern for those that followed, Welwyn Garden City, Hampstead Garden Suburb and all the post-war new towns which now have spread all over the country.

THE FIRST GARDEN CITY—PLAN OF ESTATE AND PROPOSED TOWN.

(NOTE.—The Plan of the Town, which has been designed by Messrs. Barry Parker and Raymond Unwin, Architects, Baldock, is, of course, subject to modification and further development.)

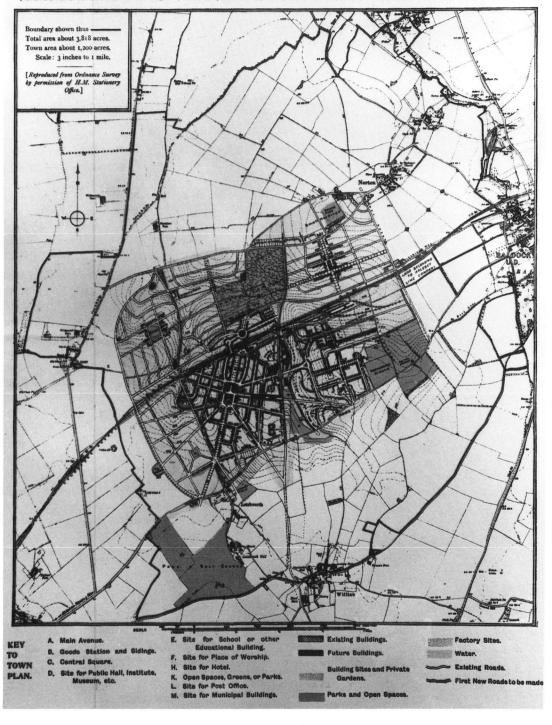

Boundary shown thus ————
Total area about 3,818 acres.
Town area about 1,200 acres.
Scale: 3 inches to 1 mile.

[Reproduced from Ordnance Survey by permission of H.M. Stationery Office.]

KEY TO TOWN PLAN.

A. Main Avenue.
B. Goods Station and Sidings.
C. Central Square.
D. Site for Public Hall, Institute, Museum, etc.
E. Site for School or other Educational Building.
F. Site for Place of Worship.
H. Site for Hotel.
K. Open Spaces, Greens, or Parks.
L. Site for Post Office.
M. Site for Municipal Buildings.

Existing Buildings.
Future Buildings.
Building Sites and Private Gardens.
Parks and Open Spaces.

Factory Sites.
Water.
Existing Roads.
First New Roads to be made

3
Somewhere to Live

The variety of styles of houses built in Letchworth at this time is remarkable, but all are clearly identifiable as 'Early Garden City' architecture. Families who had moved up from London were delighted to be in a light, spacious house with a generous area of garden. But many found it difficult to settle in their first rented house and some families moved from one road to another until they found accommodation that suited. During the early years the townspeople had to put up with the discomfort and upheaval caused as all the amenities were gradually put in place – even the delivery of newspapers caused a major headache.

There were I think two or maybe three cottage exhibitions in the early 1900s and the idea was to develop systems of building cottages cheaply for agricultural workers and people like that and the housing of the working classes. And the various patent systems were developed and they were exhibited on sites in Nevells Road, Wilbury Road and Icknield Way. One of these systems was only knocked down comparatively recently, it was a few yards up this street, Wilbury Road, on the other side it was circular, I don't know how big it was, but of course it was a bungalow type of thing and as I say it was circular with a living room, bedroom, and in the middle there was a little sort of hall which was lit from the roof that was built of some patented system of straw boarding and plastered over. It was rather ahead of its time. The very first estate office was in a pair of cottages at the top of Letchworth Lane. They knocked them together, that was the real original estate office. I don't suppose it lasted very long, it couldn't have had enough staff in there to be much good. Now this patented system, it had some name to it 'Strawnet' or something like that I think it was. It was apparently fairly substantial as long as it was looked after. I can remember it was there until quite recently, it was knocked down and a much bigger house put up. They were very generous with the land in those days. Many of the gardens are far too big really for modern requirements. This is one, but they won't let me put another place up, it conflicts with Garden City principles.

My mother said that in the early days everybody was so interested in what the other houses were like that everybody

J·E·ELEVATION

would go and see everybody else's house, but it was so muddy most of the time that whenever they went to someone's house they would take their shoes off. You got to know who was visiting, because you recognised the shoes.

I was eight years old when I came to Letchworth. My father was in business in Sandy. We lived in quite a big old house in Sandy which only had a pump and when we got here in Rushby Walk it had got taps so my brother and I nearly went mad as we were drinking water all day long. As so much needed doing in the house we went to stay with my uncle who had a nice big old house in Pixmore Way and we stayed there until the smell of paint had gone from the house.

We came to Letchworth to live in Common View in 1908 which was then Common View Square. The houses belonged to Miss Lawrence who owned The Cloisters. They were let on condition that, after twelve months, we would have to purchase them, and as my mother didn't like the house very much she decided we didn't want to purchase it, she would much rather have had one of the bungalows on the other side of the road which were then being sold for £100, but the builder decided that my father was

The opening of the Cheap Cottages Exhibition by the Duke of Devonshire on 25 July 1905.

Right: *Nos. 212, 214 and 216 Nevells Road (formerly Exhibition Road) during the 1905 Cheap Cottages Exhibition.*

Middle: *No. 106 Wilbury Road was entered by The Society of Artists into the 1905 Cheap Cottages Exhibition and was designed by Miss E. McClellon, the only woman to participate.*

Bottom: *Nevells Road – Cheap Cottage Exhibition site, July 1905.*

Left: *Nos. 6 and 8 Cross Street (the only 'Street' in Letchworth) were built by William Judges at a cost of £300 as entries in the Cheap Cottages Exhibition.*

Middle: *Another entry in the Cheap Cottages Exhibition. This house at 241 Icknield Way was built by The Fire-Proof Partition and Spandrel Wall Company.*

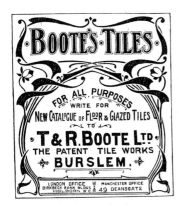

·BOOTE'S·TILES·

FOR ALL PURPOSES

WRITE FOR

NEW CATALOGUE OF FLOOR & GLAZED TILES

TO

T & R. BOOTE Ltd.

THE PATENT TILE WORKS

BURSLEM.

LONDON OFFICE   MANCHESTER OFFICE
BIRKBECK BANK BLDGS   49 DEANSGATE
HOLBORN W.C.

not earning enough wages to pay for the mortgage so he wouldn't let them have one. So we moved further up Common View to Howard Cottage Place at no.51 and there I stayed until I was married in 1929.

Oh there's a little amusing story, now I cannot guarantee it's truth, but it was told to me by a rather respected early resident, of how Letchworth is lit by water. I'll try and tell it as he told me. In the very early days there wasn't an urban district council, but there was a parish council. And some of the parish council members were also staff or something to do with the First Garden City which supplied water and gas and the street lighting was mainly, I think, entirely gas. Anyway there came an occasion when they wanted to improve the street lighting, but being a parish council they could only spend a few pence in the pound from the rates, and they'd reached their limits, so they decided they would surreptitiously put up the water rate and put up some more street lamps at the same time and that's how Letchworth came to be lit by water!

My father was an architect – he built our house in Willian Way. One of the public things that he did was the children's ward at the Letchworth Hospital which was never used as a ward. People all wondered why there were these seats in the physiotherapy room round the windows which opened up and those were for the children's toys, when it was to be a children's ward.

His forte was small houses for working people and he would discuss with prospective tenants what sort of things they wanted. And he was very popular on the council as an architect, not specially with the council, but the people used to wait to know where the houses that he had designed would be. They wouldn't go into the ones on Bedford Road, they waited for Archers Way and Monklands which he designed and they said 'I want one of Mr Tickle's houses'.

Our house didn't have a bathroom. We had a big bath in the kitchen with a big draining board over the top of it. We all had baths, but didn't have a bathroom. We used to have a fireplace there but my mother had a night fireplace put in – you kept all your tea-leaves, etc., to help keep it in all night. She used to pay 3d a week extra for that. Mind you that was taken out 20 or 30 years ago and I'm still paying 3d a week for it. All the houses were rented, you couldn't buy Howard Cottage houses.

I was born in Glebe Road and we moved to Cashio Lane, I think it cost about £400 for a semi-detached house. It backed onto Norton Road School playing ground, and there were no houses from our house up to the tiny bungalow in Cashio Lane, it was just waste scrub for quite a long time. It was a bit of low ground then and my father dug a trench to drain our garden and the soak was in this bit of waste ground. And I can remember having

Right: The cosy parlour of Miss Lee's house in Norton Way North c1908.

Barry Parker (left) and Raymond Unwin, the architects of the First Garden City.

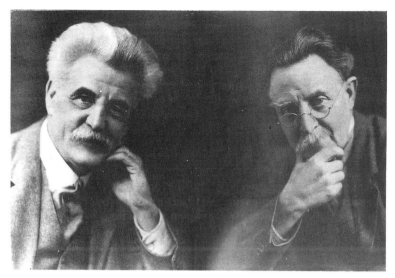

a leather helmet, I was very young, I must have been about four or five and saying I'm an airman and I dived into this blessed trench fully clothed.

There was a farm in Cashio Lane, well it was a collection of sheds really. It was attached to Payne's farm I think which was further along Croft Lane. I can remember there was a very black pond there which we used to play around and a collection of farm buildings, and old harrows and machines for sowing corn and seeds of all sorts. I remember there were little metal labels that used to dig into a reservoir of seed and scatter it and so forth. I can remember breaking these things off from these old rusting machines and using them like a catapult. Evil. And the story goes that a fully laden cart slid down into this pond and the horse was drowned and the whole lot disappeared. I don't know how true that was, I know that it was a filthy evil looking pond surrounded by elm trees, it used to stink like fury.

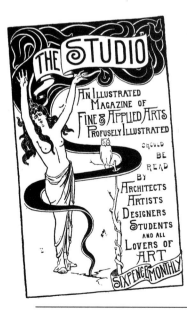

They used to make their own gas with coal and it was quite a sight to see that being done because they used to draw the furnaces in the evening, and after dark it was quite spectacular, glaring lights, and I think they used to drench the coke with water to stop it burning and it made lots of steam and we used to go along and watch them. Baldock didn't have their independent water, so the Company supplied Baldock with water as well. There was a pumping station along the Baldock Road opposite the playing fields. It's probably the only water works which has ever been burnt down! It's a tale that Bill Morton, who was the engineer, used to tell us. But it was originally a corrugated iron structure and I don't know what happened, but it all got burnt down one night. Probably they had a gas generator, it may have come from there, what they call producer gas, to drive some of the

Above: *Laneside and Crabby Corner, Letchworth Lane, built for the architects Barry Parker and Raymond Unwin. The photograph was taken pre-First World War.*

Left: *Parker and Unwin design for a group of four cottages on the Pixmore Hill estate 1906/07.*

engines – they didn't have diesels. I believe there was a steam engine there, they had about four or five pumps altogether before they finished up. And one of them was about as powerful as all the others put together, so they relied on that very heavily. But they used to keep them in commission. I think the water was about 150 feet down, in a layer of chalk which runs under London like a sort of basin. And we're more or less on the edge of it. They decided to put down another well in about the early 30s so they

brought the dowser in to begin with. He said, 'That's where the water is. Anyway they dug down there and of course they found water. They could hardly avoid it I should think. Anyway they dug a six-foot well by hand behind the same building. It wasn't very far from the earlier bore holes. And I went along with another fellow from the drawing office and they wanted some sort of invigilator to see that the test pump, which had to be done by the contractors, was satisfactory, and that meant a 24-hour spell of pumping for about a week. So we took it in turns to stay there all night. I sort of camped out so that they didn't stop. I don't think that they ever did. But it was just to see that the well was capable of delivering the quantity of water they needed. But just for the hell of it we went down in a bucket to see what it was like. It was quite interesting. They lowered a lamp as well and we stood in this bucket and down we went. Down to about 60 feet to begin with and as they pumped the water, the well became drier, and we ultimately finished up about 150 feet deep and you could look up and see the water pouring in through cracks in the chalk. It was all dazzling white chalk.

Most people in those days had penny in the slot meters for gas, the big old pennies we used to have, you'd put a penny in the slot and you'd get gas for the evening. But it became rather difficult to collect, naturally, and the meter readers used to go round with little barrows and they'd get great bagfuls of coins, stick them in these barrows which were like little cupboards on wheels, like little prams almost. They had about four or five men doing this job reading the meters. Can you imagine anybody collecting all that amount of money and just going round on foot these days? They'd come back loaded with cash.

I left school in 1930 and went to work for the First Garden City setting out roads as a young surveyor, going along with the level and theodolite and so on. The First Garden City had all its own

Workmen's cottages in Paddock Close, designed by the architect Geoffrey Lucas and awarded a prize of £25 for best group of cottages. Each group of four cost £762 11s 11d.

A heavy late fall of snow in Station Road, 24 April 1908.

utilities in those days, but I think that what really produced the revenue for the company was the electricity undertaking. A lot of people worked there – a lot more than worked anywhere else within the company. You see there were a lot of estate workers, about 20 or so at one time. There must have been 20 or 30 gas workers I suppose. There wasn't much building done by the company itself except repair work, what they used to do was let a plot on a long lease – a 99-year lease – and let the owner or builder put up houses on spec.

The company used to lay out and actually build some of the earlier roads and streets and then they would be completed to a standard and taken over by the council.

The original estate, which was about 4,000 acres, was bought in a number of different parcels over a period of about a year or so, rather in secret I should imagine. I don't know how it was done but it must have been a lot of careful negotiation I should think to do it. I think there were about a dozen large parcels in the land and then bits and pieces and the average cost would be about £40 an acre because it was nearly all agricultural. £40! That would be about £4,000 now I should think even the agricultural stuff. But it ultimately ended up with a total acreage of about 4,500 of which the town itself in the middle was about 1,500 or 2,000 perhaps. The farming land was let out to a number of farmers and one of my jobs was to look after repairs to these buildings. Local government in the early days was a parish

Above: Glebe Road c1911, out of the new roads, with its freshly planted saplings, contrasts with the mature grounds of 'Netherton' now 'Briarside' (right) on the Hitchin Road.

council, probably even just a town meeting or something of that kind. And it wasn't formed as an urban district until about 1919 or 1920. The council offices were on the top floor of the present estate office. The ground floor was occupied by the First Garden City and the upper floors by the council and, of course, that always caused a lot of confusion.

Most older residents of Letchworth will remember the time when the town had its own newspaper – The Citizen. It was started in 1906 about three years after the Garden City was founded. It was first of all printed in a house in Green Lane, the type was set by hand and the printing was done on a treadle machine. They printed a thousand copies which were distributed free to the town.

The origin came about as a result of a strike at The Garden City Press. After the strike a number of the men were not taken back again and those men got together to start The Citizen. They were L.A. Wheeler and H. Odell and A.W. Brunt, W. Reynolds and Mr. Marshall.

Eventually a company was formed under the title of Messrs Wheeler, Odell & Co. and this later became Letchworth Printers. They had works and offices in Norton Way North where the company remained until 1972.

I remember Mr Brunt telling me that they had very great difficulty delivering the papers in those days because the town was unlit and was criss-crossed with trenches and new buildings and they had great difficulty in avoiding falling in the ditches.

Workmen's cottages, Common View, c1914. The new road, as yet unlit, made newspaper and other deliveries difficult.

COMMON VIEW, LETCHWORTH.

4
People and Perceptions

Free thinkers, writers, artists, crafts people, Quakers, Theoso-phists and socialists were all drawn to the liberal society that was spreading throughout the young garden city. Those of a more orthodox persuasion thought them a little strange but largely held the opinion that variety was the spice of life, and so viewed them with tolerance and not a little amusement. And, of course, amongst these there were the personalities – men and women of vision and a sprinkling of delightful eccentrics.

Of course Letchworth had a lot of really wealthy people in it. I have been on Howard Park as a child when Ebenezer Howard stood there and said, 'Now children, come on all of you "Jerusalem" '. And we all sang 'Jerusalem' to him.

Letchworth was a very socialist place and Ebenezer Howard was as well. It was made up of the type of people who didn't believe in wars. Well, none of us do, come to that, but they used to prophesy about wars and that sort of thing you see and when the war really came, of course, there were so many conscientious objectors and they wouldn't go to war. Some were imprisoned and some were sent out in the fields to do field-work and that kind of thing. When the war was over I don't think they could face Letchworth Garden City so they all went to Welwyn.

Herbert Morrison became the Labour Home Secretary in the Second World War and he was a conscientious objector and worked in Letchworth during the First World War. He was courting a girl-friend on The Quadrant but I can't think of her name. When he got on in the world he used to come down to her house in a big car and top hat, and all this was what they were against – they didn't believe in it – but they were doing it. That was the annoying part of it. I think he opened the bridge here. That would be in the Ramsey MacDonald government – when he was a member of that.

I believe he worked on a farm in Letchworth in the First World War, he had no choice. They worked in view of the German prisoners and so did I. We used to wave to the German prisoners.

In those early days so many of the children used to run about barefoot from choice and one day, people who I think must have been newcomers said to my brothers, 'O, you poor boys, you

Cartoon by Louis Weirter, 1909, published by The Citizen and entitled, 'What some people think of us'. Outrageous stories of early Garden City behaviour abounded attracting many visitors to Letchworth to see at first hand if they were true.

haven't got any shoes,' and they gave them a pair. Of course, they were delighted, but my mother wasn't.

There were a lot of vegetarians in the early days and there was always a vegetarian shop selling wholefood. Where Burrs shoe shop is in Leys Avenue was a vegetarian shop and over it was a vegetarian restaurant. There's been a Vegetarian Society in Letchworth from almost the beginning.

There were a lot of clever people like Stanley Parker with his woodwork and writers, sculptors and various people. Well, a lot of people were attracted to the First Garden City. Well that was what attracted father here. He was involved in politics, in the

Although not many residents were drawn to the idea of 'smock and sandals' as standard dress, there were still a few who wore it. Pictured above is Andrew Muir in 'Rational Dress.'

Labour party administration. Yes, we had a bomb under the window, we were away at the time. Everyone was free to express their own views.

Letchworth was termed 'a simple life place'. Mrs Morse who lived in the last house in Wilbury Road was previously married to Mr Ironside who really was a 'simple lifer' and he used to follow the brook, which used to be at the bottom here. He would come out in a loin cloth, sandals and a crook and he would walk along Rushby Mead. One day we went into Mother and said, 'Mother, is Jesus coming?' It was just like a picture we would have seen but, of course, at a later stage we found out who it really was.

We also used to go into the common to play and there used to be a lady called Miss Black. She had the two small houses on the right hand side of Wilbury Road, just as you get round the corner from Norton Way to Wilbury Road, the two houses were one for herself and one for her cats. One day we were in the common and the boys were climbing up the trees and she came out and carried on at them alarming. She said, 'King Herod was the wisest man that ever lived.' Of course, we didn't know what she meant until we got home and told our parents who, of course, explained that he had had all the babies killed. She was Black by name and black by nature.

We always had a reputation of having a few weirdos around, people who dressed in sandals and robes. There may have been a few, I can't remember seeing any. Although there were one or two characters who gave the impression they probably would given half a chance. I remember in the early days a lot of school children going around barefoot in summer. I don't know how they did it, but I could never walk around in bare feet. But apparently some people, I don't mean poor people, thought it was good for the children's feet. And I can remember quite a few girls, particularly, going round barefoot, you know up to about six, seven perhaps eight years of age. And a lot of boys who came from farm workers families and probably they were well on the poverty line almost.

The dry town idea, that was because the lease, all the leases provided stated there should be no alcohol sold – nobody was allowed to sell anything alcoholic. Oddly enough there was alleged to be a mistake in the Conservative Club lease, they could do it for their own purposes, of course, but they couldn't sell it outside. The pub is what is now the Settlement, where they only sold tea and that sort of thing. And we had this magazine written by a man named Fitzwater-Wray, and he published this sort of skit I suppose you could call it, stories of the Knights of The Round Table, and apparently Sir Gadabout was sent to look for the holy grail or something of that sort and he came to Letchworth and he found this peculiar town with the great

The imposing Spirella building, named 'Castle Corset' in Fitzwater-Wray's detail-packed 1923 cartoon, towers over many of the town's first buildings.

Spirella up on the rock, and rows of little cottages and he encountered Sir, not Lancelot, but Sir Bidnett and Sir Benwell. Now Sir Bidnett and Sir Benwell were two architects whose proper names were Bennett and Bidwell. This was published in the early '20s I should think. It only applied to Letchworth, I don't think anybody else would have understood it.

Another person I remember hearing about was Mr Kidd. He was on the council. He decided that Letchworth needed its own cemetery as the town was growing and the churchyards were too small to cope with the town's needs. It was decided to build it by the Wilbury Road at the top of Icknield Way. And the first person to be buried in that cemetery was Mr Kidd!

My first introduction to Ebenezer Howard was when I was quite a small child and that was through the friendship of my father with him. My father was headmaster of St Ippolyts School and very often came into Letchworth and met Ebenezer Howard. A card would drop through the front door saying, 'I am coming for the weekend, from Ebenezer Howard,' and he would be there on the doorstep the next morning. We got quite used to these visits.

He nearly always had sweets in his pocket and he was quite happy with small children. So that's really where we got our first introduction to him. In those days he was on his own quite a lot and he didn't really spend his time for too long in one place as his work took him quite long distances away. But he felt he had been

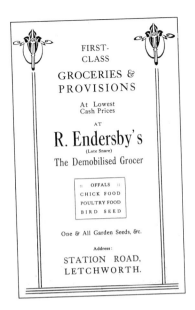

friendly with so many people. People who had children and he was friendly with the children too and although he only had a little tiny flat he gave us all a party in Homesgarth which is now Sollershott Hall. The party was in the main hall and all the flats were left open with a bowl of sweets on the table in one, a book to read in another one, probably a picture book for the smaller children and we all had a most lovely tea helped by two other gentlemen who were retired and lived in one of the flats. The one who was a retired headmaster was a bit of a humorist and came round offering us cow's juice for our tea. That of course started the party rolling and everything went with a swing.

I remember hearing about Mr William Hurst, a builder who lived in this area and went to Australia with his family, a large family, didn't do very well there, and he happened to be sitting on I think what would be called the loo, but in the garden outside, contemplating where he was going to get a good job. There was the usual newspaper hanging by his side of which he was reading a bit and saw an advertisement about Ebenezer Howard and the dream city that should be taking place and going to be built in Letchworth. He packed his family off and returned about 1903 and was one of the first builders of the town, and an interesting post script to that, he built what is now the Heritage Museum.

Mr Courtenay Crickmer was my father-in-law and in fact he was one of the first architects here. He came to Letchworth in 1904 as a young architect about to get married. He also had a friend in London who lived nearby and he was a young stockbroker, I believe. He too, was interested and as a result Crickmer came out here and eventually got a plot. The friend's name was Flemming and they had two semi-detached houses built. Now these two houses, according to Pickton and Hopes' estimate in December 1904, were going to cost £700 for the two houses.

Mr Crickmer himself was a very, very reserved man. He was a very pleasant man and fortunately I got on with him quite well, but he was very reserved and we learned very little from him about the early days in Letchworth. But we've deduced that they were in fact a very active couple in as much as they were involved a lot with the establishment of the old Letchworth Cottage Hospital and the raising of funds and that sort of thing. She was a good violinist but she was also a brilliant artist and in fact her miniatures were hung both in the Academy and the Royal Scottish Society of Watercolour Painters. I do still have one or two of those which are mainly family portraits – especially a great favourite of mine which was of her father.

Now actually the Crickmers were in Letchworth for a comparatively short time at the beginning because by the time the First World War started, my father-in-law had become quite well-known as a promising young architect and as such he was asked by the ministry, I don't know whether it was supply or defence at that time, to go up to Gretna, in the borders, because they wanted to build a town which was essentially only being built for a big munitions factory, to house the people and provide them with facilities for their living and worship.

My father-in-law became very friendly with Dr Adrian Fortescue, who was the first Roman Catholic priest in Letchworth. I don't suppose many people now really appreciate that this man was one of the outstanding men of his time – he was a genius. I don't think there's much doubt about that. Apart from being a Roman Catholic he could speak several languages, he was a painter, a very good photographer, as an amateur he wrote music, he had a great sense of fun and he was an extraordinary character, with his sense of humour and also the way he applied himself. I have a letter written by him when his housekeeper had left or retired and he's asking if Mr Crickmer's wife, with whom he had a friendly relationship, would look out for another for him. He wrote very specifically about the qualities that this poor lady must have. He starts off, 'I do not want an RC, there are great difficulties about that especially in a small country place. It is difficult for her to go to confession to her employer, also the danger is that she could become a great lady among her own class and gossip to them about all that Father does'. He goes on to add, 'Do not send me a fair young thing with her golden hair hanging down her back.' What he's saying is, 'I want someone not absolutely decrepit, but respectable in every way and capable.' And he refers to someone else and says, 'Edith says I shall have to demand most exacting references, she should be a decent cook of the kind called plain but not too infernally plain. I have suffered much from Mrs so-and-so's plain cooking which means nothing ever but cold mutton'.

Above: *Dr Adrian Fortescue, Letchworth's first Roman Catholic priest.*

Below: *Many mourners attended the funeral of Dr Fortescue, a likeable and extremely talented man.*

SCHEDULE OF PRIZES.

The FIRST SHOW

OF THE

Garden City Horticultural Society

TO BE HELD ON

MONDAY, AUGUST 6TH (BANK HOLIDAY), 1906,

AT GARDEN CITY,

On Ground Corner of Letchworth Lane.

ATHLETIC SPORTS

WILL BE HELD DURING THE AFTERNOON.

A GRAND CONCERT Will be given in the HOWARD MEMORIAL HALL

DANCING WILL TAKE PLACE IN THE EVENING ON THE SHOW GROUND, AFTER SEVEN P.M.

The Bedford Town Silver Prize Band

WILL ATTEND.

Refreshments by Mr. A. NEWTON, Baldock.

THE SHOW WILL BE OPENED AT ONE P.M.

Admission 6d., Children half-price.

Entries close August 1st, 1906.

The other thing I was mentioning about Fortescue and his sense of humour and his art too, was that he wrote music, some of it quite serious, the tunes, etc., and some of it rather different. I have one written to a hymn tune in Latin with a translation. It says, 'I am Anglo-Catholic, the thought of Popery makes me sick, to be low church is bad I think, and all dissenters simply stink!'

Courtenay Crickmer won innumerable prize competitions for designing cottage housing, as they called it in those days. Mr Crickmer was of course a townsman and when he came to Letchworth he decided that he would try being a countryman and so among other things he thought it would be a good idea to have some chickens. So he ordered some and eventually they rang him from the halt, as it was then, to say that there was a crate of chickens clucking away there waiting for him. He quickly constructed a pen in the garden fairly near the oak tree and went down to the halt with a wheelbarrow and put the crate on the wheelbarrow and pushed it back from there to Baldock Road across, of course, virtually a track, because all the houses were down in Baldock Road and the station wasn't built in those very first years of 1905/6. He got them home and put the chickens in the pen and they bedded down for the night. When he got up in the morning, lo and behold no chickens. Looking up he saw that the chickens had decided the oak tree saw far more comfortable than the pen and had flown up. He, of course, had not been enough of a countryman to know either he had to put a top to the pen or do something to the chickens!

Charles Lee was one of Letchworth's pioneers and I knew him as well as anybody. I knew his second wife Olive very well because of her interests in art, music, nature and so on, that was her sole life, cooking meant nothing to her, for herself or for Charles. I remember she went to Aldburgh. I probably took her to the station, Charles' dinner was on the stove, very small stove, in the saucepan, one onion boiling away. I had the presence of mind to turn it off! And that was Charles' dinner for the next fortnight. But he had to scrape for himself.

He was a very scholarly man in that he wrote books, several books. He associated with Wyndham Lewis on a book called 'The Stuffed Owl – An Anthology of Bad Verse' which was a book recognised by the literists. He wrote them with C. B. Perdoms. The pioneers were quite eccentric people.

There were quite a few conscientious objectors here in Letchworth. And according to the tale I've got they used to hide, when the police came for them on Letchworth Common. The Council had gates put up on the common and the nurseryman that lived in Baldock Road, by the name of Kidd, he destroyed the lot because they used to chain the gates up at night and he confronted them with it that it was illegal to do that, because it was common property. That's the gates on Icknield Way and the gates in Norton Way and he destroyed the locks or the chains or whatever. There was quite a to-do about it. They had to leave them open, unlocked, it was common property.

Yes this is about in the early days when we were young lads, my brother and myself, five or six. The Rector of Letchworth at the time was Father Olivier, the father of Lawrence Olivier, the actor, and a great friend of the family was Sybil Thorndike, later to be called Dame Sybil Thorndike. Larry or Lawrence Olivier was at school – he was older than I was – he was at a private school somewhere out in the country, we used to see him coming around the town during the holidays and breaks from school.

At that time my mother was caretaker of the Church Rooms in Commerce Avenue, it was a church hall where they had every sort of meeting you wished to have. Dances on Saturdays, rummage sales, meetings, God knows what. Dame Sybil Thorndike was very keen to get dancing going as a means of raising a bit of cash for the Church and I can remember her on many occasions playing the piano at the Church Rooms, very distinguished woman she was. I always recall her, I can see it now, I always called it her Queen Mary outfit because it was a pale blue flimsy dressy sort of outfit. The vicar, Father Olivier, lived in the rectory down Letchworth Lane and for one Christmas, Dame Sybil Thorndike gave me a beautiful leather bound book, The Arabian Nights, and my brother the Pilgrim's Progress and she autographed it, put her best wishes inside it to both my brother and myself and I often regret not keeping it, I don't know what happened to it at all. Probably Mum gave it away, she usually did.

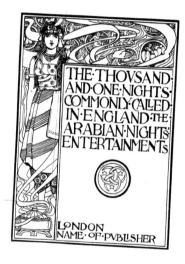

There was a lot of funny people walking about Letchworth in the early days. You would never be surprised at the number of people who walked about with monk's habits on and sandals – it was really amazing. Another very interesting person, very awkward person too I think, was Miss Lawrence who lived at the Cloisters. She had a hearing trumpet and if she didn't want to hear what you were saying she would take it away and then if you said something she would say, 'I heard that!' It was rather funny really, but she encouraged the most weirdest sort of people up to the Cloisters. We thought they were weird. Instrumentalists, people standing about reading poetry to one another, all sorts of things. She had a lovely lot of open days.

Captain McMichael lived on Norton Way, he was for animal rights. He used to upset the circus people. I was there at the circus that night and some of the circus hands got hold of him, tipped him up and his money rolled out of his pocket. They ejected him. He tried to let the lions out. He tried to do good. He tried to do various things. There used to be a fellow lived in one of the old cottages in Norton Village, he had got a dog or two in a

hut in the allotments at the back of Harrison's Nursery down Norton Village, and this dog was virtually starving to death and I know they made a court case of it, always remember that.

One woman used to dance, naked almost on the common in the dew in the early mornings, she's still about. Some of these people used to roost in the trees, so it was said. I don't know if it was true or not. There were some cranks, there certainly were. Going about in weird clothes too. The actress Margeretta Scott used to live in Wilbury Road.

One of the characters in the street was old Mr Dowling. You'd all disappear when he was about because he used to go funny when the moon was out. 'Daddy Dowling is about' and you'd run inside. He's dead now. Mrs Maynard was another character of the street. She was quite an educated lady but I've never, ever been in such a dirty house as hers. She had a funny little sweet shop. If you had ½d to spend you'd go in there, it was worth ½d just to look at it. She had sacks around her shoulders. Filthy black hands. It's a wonder we didn't all get the fleas. Across the road was Mrs Foad the faggot lady. She used to cook her faggots and chitlings (pigs insides) on a great witch's cauldron outside. There was a fish and chip van that came around. And on the Sunday the man would clean it out and take us all to Southend. We'd all stink of fish and chips. I can't remember his name. Mr Chapman, now he was funny. He used to go to his front door and blow his whistle. There was one mad dash of kids to his door to answer that whistle. The first one would get to run an errand. He used to give good tips. I remember one lady I ran an errand for. She gave me a slice of bread and jam. My mum, she was furious. 'I don't mind my kids running errands for you but don't give them no food!' That was an insult to give someone bread and jam. We used to say, 'Lets go and look in Chapman's dustbins.' The things you got out was unbelievable, little ornaments, not what you'd call rubbish. And this was continuous! Mrs Keegan, the Irish lady, she'd sit behind her curtain and wait until a ball went into her garden. She'd be out like a shot and she wouldn't let you have it back. She was nasty. When the old fish man came around we'd say, 'Can we have ½d of scrumps?' He'd say, 'Don't you want vinegar and salt!' Scrumps were the odd bits.

I remember going many years ago one Sunday evening with my father and family to the rear of where the Wilbury Hotel is now to watch Mr Irvin take off in his biplane. But, 'course being a Sunday evening, my Father was wearing his bowler hat and when he revved up the engine for this take off, away went Father's bowler hat for quite a distance and he had to run after it.

When I was at the garage another very interesting person that I met and got very, very close to really through work was Mr Irvin,

Lesley Leroy Irvin, the parachute manufacturer. When he first came to Letchworth he bought a car out of our garage, it was an Austin 7 and he progressed from that to a huge Buick, a double 6 Daimler and a 16 cylinder Cadillac. He got a yacht down in Southampton and we used to supply a driver to take him and the family down there because he didn't like driving too big distances. A most interesting person he was. I did it on one occasion – drive down to Southampton. He liked to get down there and get round the old pubs in the dingier part of the town where he'd do party pieces (before he came to England from America he worked as a circus acrobat) and one of the party pieces in these pubs, I can see him now, was standing with his head on the piano stool and playing the piano upside down. His daughter, Virginia, and his wife, took a full part in anything that was going on in the town and they would lend a hand to anything. They were very, very good. He was a most generous chap in a very quiet sort of way, he would never let anyone know what he was giving but we had a lot to do with Irvin, it was great.

I remember the scramble at the time when war was looming up and he realised, he'd got factories in Germany and France at

Left: May Day was a very popular town event. Crowds turned out on a fine May Day in 1916 to watch the crowning of the May Queen.

Below: Pre-First World War May Day procession in Leys Avenue.

MAY FESTIVITIES 1909
GARDEN CITY

this particular time so he had lots of the work people from Letchworth shipped over to France and Germany to pick up the tools and that to bring back because he knew the way things were going. It was quite an experience really.

Then there was Jack Prutton, the Communist. He was a man that was feared by all First Garden City Directors. When they used to have their Annual General Meetings – it was mainly Directors from London. One I can remember was Ralph Edge – he came from London. Another one was Dr MacFadyen's brother – he was a cripple and he was from London. When they came down and the Agenda was done the first thing they used to say was, 'Has Jack Prutton got anything in this Agenda?' and they said, 'Yes'. 'Oh'. He used to tie them up – he used to win a lot. He was a very good bloke. He was a very intelligent man. He was the Union top man. He was 100% Communist. There was a lot of those in Letchworth before the war.

Claude Sykes was a well-known character in the town and was the Speaker Finder for the Rotary Club for a long time. He was an authority on cats and used to officiate at the cat shows. He was capable of doing that. He was eccentric. He wrote a novel and he had a theory that Francis Bacon wrote Shakespeare! His wife was an actress originally.

Ebenezer Howard standing in front of the Garden City banner at the Coronation celebrations in 1911.

"CORONATION" LETCHWORTH. 1911.

The Den, now 'The White House', built for the artist C. J. Fox.

I think there was some vague thing about him being involved with some Government work which was on the secret side. I don't know what that was all about. I think some people thought that Claude Sykes was a spy! But he had his fingers in so many pies. I liked old Claude though and got on well with him.

5
The Settlement and The Cloisters

Although there was a strong country-wide temperance base in the churches, those who liked the odd drink thought it quaint to have a completely alcohol-free town. The citizens of Letchworth, however, coped very well with the situation . . . one way or another. The original non-alchoholic pub – The Skittles Inn – became a centre for educational and social activities, adding on extra dimension to early Garden City life.

My mother longed to live in Letchworth, – my father was working there after the First World War. The chance came in 1928, when a group of people from the Settlement came to Arlesey for an evening of talk and entertainment. They sang sea-shanties, 'Spend my money on Sally Brown', which tickled my mother, this being her sister's name. The warden was looking for a resident couple to be caretakers, with the man working full-

Top Right: A force to reckoned with – The British Women's Temperance Association c1912.

Bottom Right: The Fox at Willian, pictured before the First World War, was the object of many a walk from alcohol-free Letchworth.

Garden City Sports

Under the auspices of The Garden City Horticultural Society,

Bank Holiday, August 6th, 1906,

TO BE HELD IN THE

Sports Field, near the Old Post Office,

Letchworth Corner.

NOVEL AND VARIED PROGRAMME.
Sixteen Events. Valuable Prizes.
Adult and Junior Competitions.
FIFTEEN MILES WALKING HANDICAP.

Costume Cycle Parade.

BEDFORD TOWN SILVER PRIZE BAND.

Dancing from 7 p.m.
Grand Evening Concert.

Admission to Flower Show and Sports, SIXPENCE.
CHILDREN HALF-PRICE.

time in the factory. It was a tough life: Father had to stoke the central heating, look after the large garden, fruit trees and outside area, and help my mother with the cleaning.

The flat upstairs was pleasant, but there was no kitchen, so we ate our dinner downstairs in 'The Classroom', next to the kitchen, and carted stuff upstairs for the evening meal.

The Settlement had been purpose-built as a refreshment house, with a sign-board, 'The Skittles Inn'. In the attempt to return to Merrie England it had a skittle-alley, and a great inglenook fireplace. But quiet Nevells Road was not central, and, most inhibiting of all, no alcoholic liquor was sold in Letchworth. The workers took themselves off to the 'Three Horseshoes' at Norton, 'The Two Chimneys' at Wilbury, or 'The Fox' at Willian. The 'Skittles' was re-located near the station, and renamed 'The People's House.'

The building was acquired by the Educational Settlements Association, with the idea of bringing education and culture to the working classes. The skittle alley became a hall, inconveniently long and narrow; doors slid back on one side to reveal a stage. There was a pleasant common room, a large lecture room, and a small classroom. There must have been plenty of money when it opened, as the first warden lived in the Broadway and sent his children to boarding school *and* he had a paid assistant.

The high-minded and good-hearted pioneers had great ideas about extending education to the under-privileged. But you would have looked in vain for the man from the work-bench, or his wife, attending the French circle, or the ladies' leatherwork class on a Friday afternoon. I did once talk to a bewildered young woman peering blankly at a volume of Chaucer she had been given, in the hope of imbibing some culture.

But the bulk of the early members seemed to be educated people; school teachers featured largely; it was more a club for the intelligentsia, and a fascinating crowd they were to us. My parents, though naive in some ways, were intelligent, with a sound village common-sense. They sympathised with the Settlement ideals, but laughed at the lack of realism; much of it was a foreign language to ordinary people – a supper was being organised, and various 'hors d'oeuvres' discussed; My father was puzzled about these 'horse turds'. He got raked in to work the magic lantern for village lectures. The young assistant warden, Mr Porteous, whom my parents thought rather silly and improvident, (left the lights on all night and didn't lock up') tried to convey the beauty of the nude to my mother, in the cause of art. But she had her sweeping to do, and pointed out that as a former nurse she had plenty of acquaintance with naked bodies, and corpses too, if it came to that!

The first warden left, and the job was taken on by Miss Pym. My mother told me she was 'a woman with a BA.' In her time she

had refused to pay rates, since women were denied a vote, and some of her goods were distrained, including a silver teapot.

The Settlement certainly knew how to put on a show, in the form of the Summer Pageant. Long after we left, Miss Pym invented a part for me. The pageant took place, weather permitting in the garden, and it had its own conventions. The railway line ran above the garden end; whenever a train ran by, or they were busy with a bit of shunting, the actors 'froze', and came to life again only when the noise ceased.

One year we had a gypsy pageant, where elderly ladies rehearsed what were meant to be wild Hungarian dances, ending with a twist and flinging of the arms. One of these landed on my ear and sent me spinning, stunned, across the room. Then there were 'tableaux vivants', where characters were posed in a setting to look like paintings by Gaugin or Degas, or a Greek marble frieze. Maidens tugged a flower-bedecked bull to a temple while Evan Fletcher, looking Byronic, recited Keats' 'Ode to a Grecian Urn'!

Amid all the entertainment, we became aware of sombre things: men and women with foreign names and accents were brought along and made welcome, and these, I was told, were 'refugees'. Russell Scott, who promoted the Esperanto classes, took several into his home. When unwelcome war-workers and evacuated teachers were dumped upon householders, they found a meeting-place and relaxation in the common room. Bewildered Indians, kitted out in navy suits, and training at the Government Centre to be artificers, had a social evening laid on for them. My mother took me along, aged 16, and the Indians and I found it an eye-opener. They were astonished that a decent white girl should be allowed to dance with them; I was surprised to hear that a society existed where it was forbidden.

A little money was made by renting out the premises to various groups. I was intrigued by the spiritualists, and lurked

The Skittles Inn c1908. Only alcohol-free drinks were served here, and the only beer was ginger.

around hoping to see something unusual. They were mostly quite ordinary, but mother did cope now and again with the odd hysterical case.

The caretaking work proved too much for her, and after four years we left. But we kept up our membership as a family and I went to this and that until my college years. In fact, at a university interview, Mary Stocks, Principal of Westfield College, kept me talking about the Settlement. We had friends and acquaintances all over the town, who enriched our lives. There cannot have been many factory workers who kept a newspaper cutting about England's purchase of the Codex Sinaiaticus; but then, we knew Douglas Cockerell, chosen to bind it. One morning Bernard Shaw himself walked in, looking for someone, and my mother recognised him at once by his whiskers. Though we sometimes laughed at their ways, we were aware that these various people, Fabians, vegetarians, agnostics, atheists, Quakers, Anglo-Catholics, Esperanto enthusiasts, pacifists, morris dancers and lino-printers, really did look on all men as equal. My parents were never condescended to as caretakers, but regarded as friends and fellow-workers. When I came to live in the North, my students surprised me by strong feelings of 'them and us'. Certainly some people in Letchworth had more money than others; but at the Settlement you would not have known it from their clothing or ornaments; they walked or rode bicycles, and used the same forms of address to everyone. My students

The Settlement, formerly The Skittles Inn, became a social and educational centre, with an enthusiastic amateur dramatic group. The Settlement Players are pictured here in the late 1920s.

W. A. 'Bill' Furmston, energetic manager of The Skittles Inn, which was later renamed The People's House when it moved to Station Road in the '20s.

tried to convince me, but it was useless. The Settlement had demonstrated democracy and equality, and imprinted it upon me too early for any change.

I remember Bill Furmston who was the manager of the People's House. Of course they used not to sell alcohol. They used to go up the town to get drinks and that sort of thing and on the way back they would ask for tickets to the 'Holy Land'. Letchworth was called the 'Holy Land' in those days as it was so many years before they could get alcohol.

The Furmstons lived at the Skittles Inn. It was an adult education centre and a meeting place. It was non-alcoholic, well Letchworth was, that's why everyone had a dog, to walk them over the fields to Willian.

I used to go to the Methodist Church, not far from Paddock Close. There was a man come and gave a lecture on alcohol. Well he brought some sections of the body that had used alcohol a lot and it show you those veins and everything and they'd all dried like a little bit of twitch. That put me off, I've never had nothing since.

Letchworth being the town well known for having no pubs had a referendum every few years to see if the electorate wanted licensed premises and I well remember the minister of the Methodist Church, Rev William Busby, travelling around the town in his Ford car preaching about the evils of drink and it was not until well after the War that we had our first licensed hotel. It was always surprising to me we did not have a pub as Letchworth always appeared to be a town of secret drinkers, and if you stood on any of the approach roads into the town on most days you would see a constant flow of brewers' drays and wagons coming in to deliver the beer to people's houses around the town.

The Cloisters, Miss Annie Lawrence's Open Air School, was started in 1906. It was, and still is, regarded as a unique building. Architecturally quite flamboyant, many types of material were used in building it including various marbles. It was designed with the idea of making an open air life possible with many features allowing for the circulation of fresh air.

Annie Lawrence was the sister of Lord Pethwick Lawrence, and they both had a great interest in women's suffrage, and, of course, in furthering women's rights. Annie Lawrence's great interest in life was adult education. She organised many courses at the Cloisters, handicrafts, music – there was at one time quite a magnificent organ in the vestibule and the organist's name was Frank Merry. She was also a pioneer of men and women studying together, attending courses together and swimming together – so much so that there was no separate dormitory accommodation for residential courses – all the participants would sleep in

THE CLOISTERS

The Cloisters built by Annie Lawrence as an open-air school and centre for crafts and adult education.

hammocks with only a very flimsy curtain between males and females, hence the jokey reputation that the permissive society began in Letchworth in 1906 – not an historical fact, I think, but one of the things that people attached to the place with the reputation of the Cloisters. Apart from the fact that this was a unique aspect, Miss Lawrence took adult education very seriously – so much so that people from local industry would go in the evening for many of the activities I have mentioned, but there would also be ordinary educational subjects such as English and Arithmetic – a forerunner of the Technical College that we know today.

My first school was run by Miss MacFadyen, the sister of one of Letchworth's general practitioners. It was an excellent little school in which both Ethel Henderson and Beatrice Holloway taught. Once a week we went to the Cloisters, the boys for printing and many other useful crafts and the girls mainly for weaving. Miss Lawrence was a disciple of William Morris.

In the summer, Miss Lawrence was generous with her lovely little swimming pool, built, I suspect, to resemble a bathing pool of ancient times.

I came to Letchworth in 1937 to teach physical education and one of the main interests I think was the swimming which took place

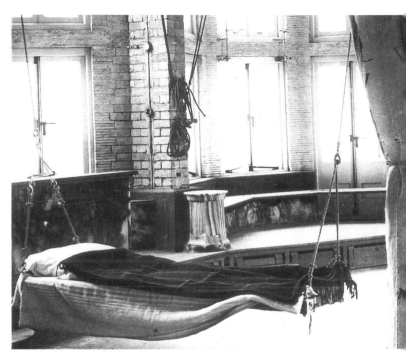

Above: *Fountain and organ at The Cloisters.*

Right: *The Cloisters, where residents slept in hammocks let down from the roof.*

in the Cloisters, under the 'eagle-eye' of Miss Annie Lawrence who owned the building. The swimming bath was modelled on an old Roman bath, circular with a sort of fish-tail at one end.

It was cleaned out I think about once a fortnight and when it was clean it was very, very cold the children said. I didn't actually go in to see. One of the main attractions there was that every child who learned to swim in her pool was presented by Miss Lawrence with a fountain pen.

On Sunday the Wall's ice-cream 'Stop me and buy one for a penny' was always there and of course there was the beauty of the gardens and her swimming pool and climbing the spiral staircase to the top of the tower to have a good view of the whole area.

I remember the bandstands on the Broadway and the bandstand in the common, both no longer there. We used to go there or to the Cloisters for Sunday afternoon concerts. Everybody that was anybody used to go there on Sunday afternoons. It was really lovely that was. Miss Lawrence used to collect rents from my mother-in-law in Ridge Road, she used to go there with her trumpet in her ear and say, 'Mrs Bilson, any club this week, can you afford to put a shilling on your club card this week?' She was a wonderful old lady, deaf as a beetle, bit like me now.

The pool was cleaned out and clean water put in on Monday morning. But I'm quite sure we didn't swim on a Sunday I don't think that was done. It would take the day anyway to empty it

Above: *Lunch at The Cloisters c1908.*

Left: *'The Masque of the Leech', performed at The Cloisters in 1914.*

and scrub it out. We used to go down there twice a day. The Cloisters was the highlight really, I've no doubt about that, and of course Miss Lawrence was an idealist and she got people there who she thought would be idealistic as well. And that hall was open and the band played in the open air because for some reason or another it always seemed to be nice weather, when we were small.

I was very keen on Greek dancing, which was something that the children hadn't done before. It was arranged that we should have the Greek dancing lessons in her hall which was circular with pillars. There was just one problem – she didn't like to see the children dancing round in a circle because it made her feel giddy, so if she arrived the main way to get rid or poor Miss Lawrence was to send the children around the room. But it was very pleasant there.

6
Earning and Spending

The early Garden City demonstrated just how resourceful people could be. Houses were springing up, but there was not yet the variety of shops to meet all the demands. So the streets filled with delivery men, who, identifying a need, sought to satisfy it. Housewives and widows saw a way of supplementing their income by selling sweets, cakes and other delicacies from their front rooms. And businessmen took advantage of this young, vibrant society by opening shops and factories which soon thrived and became small communities themselves. The Co-op, as one would expect, played an important roll in this strongly socialist town.

In 1905 – right in the beginning, my father, C.F. Townsend, was Joint Secretary of the Resident's Council. He founded Letchworth Laundry in 1909. He designed the building I think, because he was an architect as well as all the other things he did. He also designed all the machinery in it and was responsible for all the chemicals that were used because he was an analytical chemist as well, so he actually knew about everything that went on. He was the founder along with Mr Jackson who later on took it over. My father was also a freelance journalist and the editor of a trade magazine called 'The Power Laundry'.

THE ARDEN PRESS

LETCHWORTH

My mother worked for W. H. Smith & Sons' bookbinding works in London and came to Letchworth in 1908. At this time the firm was developing its wholesale and retail trade and the now familiar shops began to open. It was also decided to open a combined printing and binding works at Letchworth which would incorporate the artistic ideals of William Morris and the arts and craft movement into commercial book production as well as the growing advertising industry in which W. H. Smith had long had an interest. It was this development that brought my mother, Elene Zompolides to Letchworth in 1908. She came to work as an artist/designer in a combined bookbinding works and Arden Press when Douglas Cockerell was transferred as the controller of the bindery from London. He was said to be England's greatest bookbinder and his reputation has never been superseded.

My father came to Letchworth in 1908 to manage the Co-op, which in those days was a two-fronted shop in Leys Avenue. The

Above: *The opening of the
Co-operative Stores in Leys
Avenue in 1907.*

Left: *In 1913 building was
begun on larger premises in
Eastcheap where this interior
shot was taken in the late
1920s.*

top of the building is just the same as it was then. And the first
part of the Eastcheap building was put up and opened in 1913.
The Co-op was very strong in Letchworth – both socially and as a
shop. And you see, there was the coal business. That was started
during the First World War. And the bakery was put up before
the end of the war in Commerce Avenue. It was quite a big
bakery and it was very good bread, I can assure you! The rest of
it went up in stages between the wars in Eastcheap.

The last thing my father dealt with was the dairy and now of
course it's all gone – which is very sad.

I helped with the Co-op Junior Guild and the Co-op Junior
Guild's Concert Party which was very successful. I used to copy

out all the words of the songs so that they could learn them. Well, my husband played for them, you see. And I helped make the costumes and look after the costumes, because we used to give several concerts a year, not only at the Co-op, we always did two a year at the Brotherhood Hall, because they had a concert every Saturday night between the wars. We went out to various villages, to Knebworth and Ashwell and Stotfold and Shillington – we went to all of those, at different times.

In those days of course it looked as if Letchworth at one time was going to be an important place in the motor industry. The Lacre Car Company started their business in Works Road. They used to make motor cars and lorries which were used for road sweeping purposes. Then there was the Phoenix Motor Company in Pixmore Avenue and they used to make a very nice little private car.

There was Heatly-Gresham, an engineering company, The Lorraine Works, an embroidery works – that was developed by two Swiss people. They had two factories, one on each side of Works Road.

Then of course there were various printing firms. J. M. Dent had a big factory on Dunhams Lane and they used to print the Everyman series of library books and had their own electrical plant producing their own electricity. There was a little brook that ran down from the factory under the railway line out into what was then Icknield Way and there used to be some very smelly effluent going down there from this electrical plant. Then the Garden City Press had their place in Pixmore Avenue, and Letchworth Printers were in Norton Way.

The Spirella Company came in 1911. They had a wooden building on the site where the school huts in Nevells Road used to be at first and then they had their permanent building put up on the other side of the road. One of the things I remember about the Spirella Company – the original plan of Letchworth showed a road from what was the Country Gentlemen's Association building down to the rest of Nevells Road at the bottom, but the Spirella Company insisted on having their site in Bridge Road and so that idea fell through – there wasn't an extension of Nevells Road up to the C.G.A. That's the reason why so many of the numbers at the bottom of Nevells Road are in the 200s – the numbers started at the C.G.A. building up in Icknield Way.

Meredew's came in 1912 – I remember them coming because many of their employees came with them and several of them came to live in Common View, that was when the rest of Common View Square was developed to make houses for some of the Meredew's employees.

For our clothes, we used to support Rawlinson's which was where the Supasnaps shop is now and Spink's & Son men's shop towards the bottom of Leys Avenue. For our grocers, we used to go to Snare's in Station Road, we got our bread from Charles Wright in Leys Avenue – there used to be several bakeries in the town in those days – Wright's and Nott's and the Co-op and Essex in Station Place. There was also another men's shop in Station Place called Pugh's – that used to be the more expensive place.

Foster & Scott's was about the second shop to open in the arcade in Letchworth, the first one being Claude Hartley's father who opened a china shop in 1924 or something like that.

All the shops in the arcade were taken and it was quite a centre for doing some good business and it had the added advantage on a wet day that people could shop in comfort, providing it wasn't like a wind tunnel coming from Leys Avenue into Station Road.

One of the early manufacturers who came to the town was the Marmet pram factory, which was started in 1913, surely the Rolls Royce of all perambulators. The owner, Mr Morris, lived with his family in the Glade in the later years. Of the shops, the first shop in Letchworth was owned by Mrs M Beddoe in Station Road just below the entrance to the Wynd. She sold newspapers, confectionery, cigarettes and tobacco. In 1907 the Co-op came to the town. A small building was built in Leys Avenue. Russell's first chemist shop was opened in Station Road and later a second one in Leys Avenue. Fred Nott opened a bakery and two cafés, one in Eastcheap, built in 1909 and the Willow Café in Leys Avenue. The much-loved Icknield Halls were opened in Eastcheap where dances and dinners were held regularly, they

The first shop to be opened in Station Road was occupied by the post office in 1905. This photo was taken c1910.

were also much used for charitable functions, Rotary luncheons and Masonry dinners, and were greatly missed when they were closed down. Fortunately the Plinston Hall was built on the site of the old Grammar School assembly hall and has taken the place of all public meetings and entertainments. Ken and Lesley Spink's came to the town from Great Dunmow, and Ken owned a fine drapers shop, which served the town well for many years. His brother Lesley had a men's outfitters across the road, both shops being in Leys Avenue. Lesley Bennett was a Ford car dealer and he had a garage near the People's House in Station Road, he did much civic work for the town and his brother, Morris, opened a high class jewellers shop in the arcade, now run by his son John. Claude Hartley opened a glass and china shop, originally in the arcade but now in Leys Avenue, run by his son Peter. Several of Hitchin's well known stores came to Letchworth in the early days. W. B. Moss and Sons Ltd had a grocers in Leys Avenue; also a health food store for the many vegetarians that had come to the town. Also Brooker's the ironmongers had a large shop in Leys Avenue at the entrance to the arcade. Nichol's the drapers, Hitchin drapers, opened a branch in Leys Avenue entirely clothes and hats for the female sex. Sidney Thacker has a tobacconists shop at the bottom of Leys Avenue and was an early resident of Letchworth, his father being the first station master here.

Bowyer-Lowe was the man who invented the J. A. Prestwich motor-bike engine. I think he was the chief engineer at the Phoenix Motor Works – then he and some more people started a radio factory. It was just under the bridge at Spring Road. I know that's where it was because I worked there. I think it was when I was about 15.

I recall the Cheetham Brothers, they were great they were. I think one of them was a great acrobat type of bloke. I understand he appeared in the 1908 Olympics.

As kids we used to go to the Cheetham's shop for monkey nuts. He used to keep a barrel outside filled with them and he used to say 'Here you are boy – come here – come here – you don't want a bag.' He'd put his hands in and fill our pockets – we would have our pockets right down here. At the end of the cinema we were over our shoes in monkey-nut shells.

My father used to do all his deliveries on a bike – very few tradesman had vans in those days – and I've known him to bike from Letchworth to Langford with a 7/6d wreath – he'd got to make the frame with the moss, buy the flowers , make the wreath and deliver it for 7/6d. It just shows you how things were in those days – how hard they had to work and I remember when Ebenezer Howard died my father worked 36 hours straight off making wreaths.

Nott's Bakers, Eastcheap, with six different delivery vehicles.

I was born in Letchworth in 1918 and my father came to Letchworth in 1916 during the First World War to work at the Kryn and Lahy factory on armaments. Eventually my father left K & L and started his own business in Letchworth, which was in ladies and gents shoes and shoe repairs, but before starting the shop it was a usual thing in Letchworth for many of the small, private houses to have their own shop in the front room. There would be sweet shops in one street, vegetable and fruit shops in another street and goods were brought round the streets too. Hartley's would come round with a paraffin van, Mason & Casson used to come round with a milk van and you used to take out your jug to Mason & Casson to get it filled with milk. Fred Nott, his men came round with their wicker baskets with bread and we got to know all the tradesmen and we were fond of them all. Fields from Commerce Way was a popular dairy.

My father had his shop in the front room of our house as others did in those days selling sweets and tobacco. I remember a Mrs Grey had a shop in her front room in Ridge Avenue, and a few doors up Broughton Hill there was a Mrs Cafford, who had a sweet and tobacconist shop – this happened in many houses in Letchworth in the early days, but eventually shops became available in the town centre. The town centre was not very large at the time and when they were going to build a few shops in The Wynd, my father applied for one because he wanted to turn that into a shop for

ladies' and gents' shoes and the back of the shop to be a repair shop. There was also in The Wynd old Billy Furr, commonly known as Fishy Furr. One or two other shoe repair shops eventually sprang up along the Wynd – Bill Pierce and Jack Smith.

My father had been an apprenticed plumber and came to work at Brooker's in Hitchin. He then came to Letchworth and brought his father, also an apprenticed plumber. My father and his brother Bert, with £100, opened an ironmongers in Letchworth down the bottom next door to Squires' Dairy as it is now. Horses and carts in the back yard. They opened Underwood's Ironmongers in the 1930s and opened a large second shop at the top of Leys avenue. There were known as 'Top Underwood's' and 'Bottom Underwood's'.

My brother helped out in the shop and his job after school was to weigh out the bags of soda and soap flakes in the back. Paraffin was delivered in a van. In those days everything was delivered, including shopping.

Wilfred Kitchen was a well-known figure in Letchworth. He had a shop in Leys Avenue called The Embassy where he sold violins and other instruments. He and his wife lived above the shop. He taught violin as well. When he was giving violin lessons she was looking after the shop.

There used to be a lot of people that had little businesses from home. Just up Glebe Road there was a man that sold hot faggots. A beautiful smell, but I couldn't face the old stuff. You would go to his house with a plate and he'd put it on the plate and cover it with a bit of paper.

There was Sly's corner, Lucy Sly's sweet shop. Somebody called Painter's at the top of Glebe Road; a blind man, but he knew when you had given him sixpence or something like that – it was a sweet shop.

I recall the old shops – ah, those were the days. At Moss's I used to go and sit on a stool and they used to weigh everything and cut the exact size of a piece of cheese you wanted. They used to have lovely ham and pork pies. They would send their man round to the house. Old Mr Flack came round with a push-bike with the orders on. He used to come and mother always gave him a cup of coffee and he would take the order and then it was delivered. At Christmas all the customers were given a present. Perhaps a quarter of tea. And there was wonderful cheese there as well. A special Stilton. And Cheshire, for Christmas.

As a child, the first memory I have was the muffin man coming down Glebe Road with muffins on a tray on his head and the man ringing a hand bell. Another man used to come calling out bananas, two a penny or four for threepence. I used to say to mum, 'which is best?' We had Roberts the milkman, up the road, you could get most things from him.

Mr Paynter was at the end of the road. You could get cigarettes and sweets sold from the house. And another lady down the road, Mrs Brand, made toffee and Mrs Vandyke in Common View made nut toffee and that was better than ever. She gave the money to one of her charities.

We used to go to Triangle Stores. That was as far as I was allowed to go, up there. But mostly things were delivered at the door, I mean you had the International bring your order and the fish man came, Mr Calcraft, I think that was on a Thursday or a Friday. Mr Hartley came round on a horse and cart with vinegar and paraffin oil and all the other things.

In 1922 when I was seven we moved to the shop at the bottom of Station Road – my father was a florist – he was very good with flowers and he worked in nurseries before the war and used to do a bit of wreath-making and bouquets – then he started up at the shop at the bottom of Station Road. There was a fruit shop on the corner of Norton Road and on the Station Road side we had a sweet shop which was kept by my mother with cakes and cigarettes, etc.

We had a letter come one day from someone in South Africa and it said, 'To the best florist in Letchworth' and the post office

The Triangle Stores in Common View, mid 1920s.

sent it to us. My mother was more well known than my father because in the sweet shop we used to sell all the kiddies things like gob stoppers. She used to buy all sorts of cheap sweets and make them into penny bags on a Monday morning and in the afternoon us kids would go wild. After that, Monday afternoon was 'Penny-bag afternoon'. Most youngsters knew my mother. My father was a florist and better known by older people.

Mr Maclean was the sales manager for the Spirella company. He was a great golfer and used to play with a chemist, also a scout. On one occasion, while they were playing, the chemist said, 'I've made a lovely formula for tooth powder, I'd like your family to try it out.' So Mr Maclean took some and his wife and three sons tried it out. Some time after the chemist asked him what he thought about it. He said, 'It was marvellous stuff and he'd like some more of it.' The chemist said he wished that he could sell it. Mr Maclean said, 'You manufacture it, and I will market it.' And I understood that that was the start of Maclean's toothpaste.

There was real community spirit then. There used to be the May Day celebrations and all those sort of things. The Co-op used to be a big centre too in those days. Used to have this big hall – dance hall – at the top. I remember going to a Co-op Exhibition and a bloke had got some counters and he couldn't find out what they were and I told him they were 'bread' tokens. If your mother went to the Co-op and bought so many tokens when the baker came he would take them for a loaf of bread because the baker didn't take any money. Then you had the dividend. The Co-op organisation did a lot of other things apart from retailing. They did concert parties and educational activities, they did everything there. We used to go there as teenagers and there was Mrs Freeman. Her husband was the political agent for the Labour Party. She used to teach us dancing.

There was a butcher – Arthur Ansell – they were a big family, six brothers and they all took it on, one after the other. I used to have to go up there before I went to school and get two sheeps livers – they used to be sixpence each and if they charged me more, 'Back you go with them, tell them I don't want them, I just want sixpence each' – same with breast of lamb, Mum would only have a certain breast of lamb, not just any old breast, and if you went and got it . . . 'Back you go, you tell Arthur I want something decent – that's old ram', she'd say.

I came to work at Tilley's. I was under the buyer to Mr Ernest. There were two Tilley brothers. I used to go to Luton to buy the hats. I remember the Tilleys having a big evening upstairs in North Hall and all the big millinery warehouses in Luton came and showed lots of hats and there was one special hat that you had to give a name and I named it Will o' the Wisp and I won the prize and had to go to Luton to choose a hat, which I've still got.

Above: *Beddoe's newsagent and tobacconist, Station Road c1910.*

Left: *The staff of Tilley's in Leys Avenue which stocked hats, fabrics and fashions – everything for the modern Garden City woman.*

TILLEYS WINTER SALE
SEE WINDOWS—They Speak for Themselves
Phone 409.   LETCHWORTH

Co-operative Wholesale Society's fancy dress competition 1920s.

Our meat was delivered by Ansell's Butcher, Station Road, in a motor bike and sidecar. I remember the Countryside Library was at the top of Leys Avenue and it was 2d a week to borrow a book.

At Christmas time, for shopping we went to Fox's Stores (at the bottom of Leys Avenue). They stayed open until 7pm on Christmas Eve and reduced prices! The weather always seemed freezing then!

For a day trip to London we caught the early 'workman's' train to London, fare 1/9d. All the West End stores closed at midday on Saturday then. For shoe repairs we went to Mr George Barr who had a place at the back of The Wynd.

Every year the Co-op used to hold their sports because they were quite a thriving community and had a good meeting place in the town and many of these sports were held in what we call the Arena today, the Arena Parade and Eastcheap.

At the Co-op there was a big fancy dress parade all round the town and you walked to the recreation ground in Baldock Road, opposite the football club, where everybody would be given a lovely picnic tea, races would be run and prizes given. A good time had by all! I remember always going to that one.

Moss's, in Leys Avenue, had lovely polished wooden counters and we would sit up on them while our mother discussed her order with the assistant who would be dressed in a pristine, starched white apron. Long discussions would go on about relative values of various commodities. Bacon would be sliced in front of you to what thickness you required. Cheese cut with a wire, sugar and dried goods weighed into dark blue bags. I can still remember the deft way that these bags were folded over and tucked in at the top. Mother's order would be written on a pad as she dictated it and it was delivered the next day by a boy with a large basket on the front of his bicycle. Saturday evening, as a treat, and one of the few days that father didn't work overtime, we would all walk into the town where, in the winter, the shops would be brightly lit and we would buy our special Saturday night meal from the Home and Colonial store. Corned beef, or perhaps haslet, or sometimes as a special treat, ham, freshly sliced, and a wedge of dark fruit slab cake with almond icing on the top. Commerce Avenue had interesting shops, one of these, Cakebread Robey, sold plumbing fittings etc. There was a branch of John H. Green in the yard where my father had his workshop. The church hall stood half way up, next to Green's. At the end of this road there was a row of cottages where the firemen lived, just behind the fire station that was in Eastcheap. In a lane behind Commerce Avenue there was a working forge and I would often go down there to smell that acrid smell and watch the horses being shod. I would flinch when that red-hot shoe was placed on the hoof, and that strange scorching smell I still remember. At the corner of this lane in Commerce Avenue was the library, where I first learned to browse among books. Both my parents were avid

The Arcade in Leys Avenue c1920 with Brookers to the right and Tilley Bros to the left

readers and so I had good influences in that direction. The People's House, now the 'Job Shop' was an excellent and well patronised café.

There were only a few shops in the Norton Area, i.e. Triangle General Stores in Common View – Mr and Mrs Collins (formerly Beasleys') were the proprietors. Outside the stores there were slot machines vending cigarettes at 2d for 5 Black Cat and for 20 players it was 11½d. There was Norton Post Office and provisions, where the Post Master was Mr Gibbs, the wireless shop was run by Mr Reed where you took wireless accumulators for charging – that was, of course, before we had electricity. Lighting was by gas downstairs and by candle upstairs.

There were also 'in-house' shops: Mrs Painter in Glebe Road, Mrs Maynard in Common View, Mrs Cook in Cromwell Green – all selling sweets and cigarettes. Almost everything could be delivered to the door. Milk from Roberts' dairy in Glebe Road, bread from Hanscombe's bakers in Baldock. There was also a bakery between the Triangle Stores and the Methodist Church, run latterly by Goodship and Parker. Mr Softly, a grocer in Station Road, used to call for your order on one day and deliver it the next. Fremlin's used to deliver beer and Corona soft drinks and George Humm made lemonade. A fish and chip van was in Glebe Road twice a week and Ansell's, the butchers, called at the house. The deliveries were made by Len Day who later had his own shop in Station Road. Shoe repairs were no problem as nearby repairers were Sid Cooper, Common View, Mr James, Norton Road, and Mr Denman, Common View. The local greengrocer was Mr Johnson of Common View. He had a horse and cart and his seat was a box of Fyffe's bananas. Coal was also delivered by horse and cart by Mr Berry of Green Lane and paraffin and hardware by Mr Westall of Common View. Ben Parker of Norton had quite a few horse and carts and we used to collect the horse droppings for the garden.

I recall the Brolio ice-cream man, and the Wall's 'Stop me and buy one' was a tricycle with a large box in front. I also remember Mr Wilkinson making his ice-cream in a shed next to his house in Common View.

Mr Gilley in Common View started his window-cleaning business with one ladder and a hand-cart. His sons – Tom, Bill, Sid and Arthur subsequently joined him. They were very hard-working and the business grew under the watchful eye of Mrs Gilley after Mr Gilley's death.

A knife grinder used to come around on a regular basis in the mid-thirties. He had a handcart on which he sat and peddled to rotate his grind-wheels. He would sharpen knives and scissors, etc.

7
World War I

The Garden City had barely celebrated its 10th birthday when war was declared. Building work slowed up as men went off to fight and the town welcomed yet more newcomers – this time refugees from Belgium who sought work and shelter in the new town.

One night, I was lying in me bed, when we heard all the whistles going, and I was listening, and we heard this noise coming, and I got out of bed and looked through the window, because we daren't put no light on or anything. It was a moonlit night, and there was a great big cigar like thing came right over the railway line, and I thought, 'That's something that shouldn't be up there, if that's a German going to put a bomb on the gasometers . . . we'd be blown up' – and we would have done! It hung about for quite a while. And I thought they was waiting to see if they could see a light or see anything. It was a German Zeppelin! It was in the paper afterwards. You see there was no wireless or nothing. Everything came in the paper what you wanted to know. A lot of people saw it in the sky, because all the wardens and that was running round and they saw it. They had wardens just the same as they had in the Second World War. And I know that the men didn't half have a job in the First World War if anything came over, because every gas light had to be put off. There were such a lot of gas lights to be pulled down, it takes time, they couldn't just switch 'em off! A man had to go round each with a pole. And I know some nights they never even put them on if it was moonlit.

My mother came from Norfolk because her step sister was living in Letchworth, then I think she met my father. But she was the eldest of six, I think she weighed three pounds when she was born and they kept her in a shoe box with cotton wool and olive oil. I mean a small baby like that in those days had to be protected. She was a VAD nurse – Voluntary Aid Detachment, which they always called Virgins Awaiting Destruction and she became a Red Cross nurse during the First World War. She was in munitions as well, I remember laying in a ploughed field in the middle of the night seeing a Zeppelin go over. She was working in the munitions factory down somewhere, I don't remember exactly. She's also been up in one of these string and paper flying machines. There used to be a lot of army camps, Royal Flying

Corps camps around there in the First World War. When she became a Red Cross nurse she was with amputees which was a rather harrowing time for her. And of course at the end of the war she had Spanish 'Flu very badly and she lost twin boys.

In the First World War there was a 'flu epidemic, and me brother caught it, but of course he went home to Belgium and it turned to pneumonia. He died from pneumonia in the end. And Shelvoke sent down any one who was smoking so that they could smoke to keep the germs down, you see to fight the flu. People were allowed to smoke to fight the 'flu. And now they are trying to stop it. That was at the Lacre and people were allowed to smoke then.

In Letchworth, of course, there was quite a strong movement against the war. There was quite a lot of conscientious objectors and they were really run down by the people who were supposed to be patriotic. After all you can't help how you feel about a thing, can you? And to be a conscientious objector in those days you had to be a lot stronger than actually going with the flow. It was like a dirty word. I can remember being in the same class as Christine Sunderland and from time to time we had to write an essay or something like that. I think the subject was that we could write about our family, one of our family. I can remember being ever so shocked because Christine put, 'My father is a conscientious objector.' Well, she couldn't spell very well so she actually put, 'my father is a CO.' I didn't know what a CO was at that time. But, oh, she was very proud of the fact, and her mother was allowed to take them about once a month, I think, to the prison. I think it was Wormwood Scrubs he was held at. All I know is that years later when Mr Sunderland had a house built in Cashio Lane, it was a very ordinary looking door on it, and in that area quite a lot of those houses and cottages had thatched roofs and they had these big doors. I happened to say how I liked the oak doors. And Mr Sunderland said to me that if you'd been behind oak doors for, I think, four years, you'd never want to see an oak door again. Yes, he suffered.

I don't think my mother was very sympathetic towards conscientious objectors because she had members of her family in the fighting forces. Her brother-in-law and his sons got killed and her own favourite brother got killed. And it's when things happen to oneself that you do not have a lot of sympathy with people who think like that . . . I mean, actually, I should say that as far as Mr Sunderland went he suffered a lot of privation in prison, for his conscience. But other people, they thought, well, he was shirking.

I was nine when the war finished. Then there was this terrible 'flu epidemic which killed more people than those which were killed in the war. I was the first in our family to have this 'flu. My father and my sister nearly died. They were so ill. And then there were two other members as well in the family that had it. I took

it home and I had it the longest. I won't say I had it the most severely, but I did have it the longest. I can remember that I almost had to learn how to walk again when I got out of bed I was so weak. My hair was coming out in handfuls and my stockings were all hanging loose on my legs. So I was pretty ill.

When it came to the armistice my sisters went into town and I was left behind as I hadn't yet recovered. And they came back all excited and they said, 'Oh there's a huge bonfire being built in the town. Everybody's bringing rubbish and there's perambulators and all sorts of things.' And they said it was marvellous. The bonfire was going to be lit because the war was over. And I wasn't allowed to go because I hadn't really recovered from the 'flu. Oh I thought it was awful. I'm always being done out of something. I watched it from my house. I watched this great flare and the fireworks. We lived on Wilbury Road at that time and there weren't the buildings that there are now. You could clearly see the Spirella building. That was about the nearest building. This glow from the bonfire was more or less in that direction. The whole sky was lit up and there were fireworks and everything. I can remember my mother wrapping a shawl around me as we both stood looking out of the window at it. Of course when my sister and my father came home I thought, 'I wish I'd been there'. I can remember it so very, very clearly.

After the war it was hard for a lot of the pupils at school, because their fathers, or some of them, were killed and these poor little things used to wear black bands round their arms and the

Territorials leaving Letchworth Station in the First World War

Belgian workers at the Kryn and Lahy.

girls used to wear black ribbons on their hair. There were those that came home. A lot of them were out of work. Didn't have any jobs. It was the same everywhere. It was like that here as well. And then, I didn't know when this was, whether it was in 1920 or what, there was a big procession in Letchworth and it was all to do with the League of Nations.

And I can remember Dad, too, talking about when the Zeppelins came over Letchworth. Ferris, who was the caretaker of the fire station, never put the alarms up to call the firemen out. He ran out to the houses banging on the doors calling, 'Come on, the buggers are over! The buggers are over!' They were saying they could hear it 'woo, woo woo' over the top and they said they saw, actually saw, I can't believe it myself, they said they actually saw the Zeppelin that was set on fire by Lief Robinson at Cuffley – they saw it burning in the sky. They might have done, I doubt it.

What I can remember was all the horses up Pixmore Way. That was just meadows on both sides and you could smell Pixmore Way from about a mile away from home – you could smell these horses before you ever got to them. That's the only thing that sticks in my mind about the First World War. They were army horses. And the guns, they were all stacked up there. There were all fields there.

Then of course the First World War came along and many things changed. There were lots of Belgian refugees came to live in the town. We had some living with us at various times. Lots of the people of Letchworth of course took in Belgian refugees and eventually the Westbury Estate was built specially to house them – it used to be called Little Antwerp in those days and there were quite a number of them who worked at the Kryn & Lahy factory. The Belgian man who lived with us used to work there – sometimes he would be there for 48 hours straight off. He used to work on the blast furnaces and when they were heating them up he would have to stop for a long period.

We had one Belgian stay with us. He was walking about up the road and he had nowhere to go – my mother was paying the milkman – and he came up to my mother and he asked her if she knew where he could get in because he had nowhere to go and she took him in. His name was Verreyt. In his own trade he was an architect at Malines in Belgium. He worked at the Kryn – they all had to work at the Kryn – hundreds worked there.

I knew an old Belgian lady called 'Granny' and she used to come to the butcher's shop when we were in there. She said, 'English people are the laziest people going – absolutely lazy – none of them carry their shopping home – they all have to have it sent!' She termed that as very, very lazy. The Belgians had a horse flesh shop half way down The Wynd. Franklin's Pet Shop at that time was the Belgian Grocer's Shop.

My youngest brother used to play with some of the little Belgian boys who often used to smoke on the common. My mother used to say to my brother, 'Now you are not to smoke if you go and play on the common.' He said, 'No', and then one day he came back crying and he said, 'I've been smoking and I feel sick' – he never smoked again!

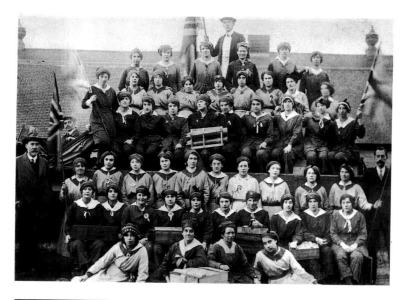

Thousands of women were employed in the munitions factories during the First World War

My husband worked at the Lacre, and that's where I met him, you see. He used to test all the lorries, take them out to see if there was anything wrong with them, and then deliver them in London, during the War. Well, when father died, all the Belgians were getting ready to go back home, they were all packing up and they were sending them home, as quick as they could. And my husband was so afraid, he used to say, 'Well if you go to Belgium with your mother, I shall lose you – she'll marry you off to a Belgian.' And my mother would say that because I was a minor – and I was only 20 then – you had to have your parents' consent to stay. So, I was crying every day. We used to go home to dinner and cry together. 'Mother will you come and sign,' I would say. And she would reply, 'I can't, I can't sign you off.' We wanted a special licence you see, because we never knew when she was going to be sent away, and that went on for about a fortnight. My mother was very friendly with Mrs Kryn, she used to go in the drawing room and have chats with her. So she told herself, 'I'll go and talk to Mrs Kryn,' thinking she might know something about my husband, and when she came back from there, Mrs Kryn must have turned my mother round, 'cos she said, 'Well, I've enquired about the boy, and Mr Shelvoke says he's a real good bloke, comes from a good family.' His mum had come from Swindon, he was lodging in Letchworth, see, that's how I met him. So one day I went home, and I said, 'Well, Mother, will you consent at last?' 'Yes,' she said, 'I will.' I never wanted any dinner, I went back to work and I was dying for my husband to come in on a lorry. I was still in the view room at the Lacre then. And I used to watch him in the view room where I could see the lorries come in from a test, and soon as I saw his lorry come in, I couldn't get out quick enough. I said, 'Oh Jim, Mother says she's willing to sign.' He went straight up to the office to Mr Shelvoke, and he said, 'Oh well, Madame DeRoeck,' that was my name, 'has consented to sign for the marriage'. So Shelvoke said, 'Bloody well take a lorry, Hacker,' he said, 'and drive 'em to Hitchin.' So off we went, the three of us, on a lorry!

The week I went to see me mother home, there on the platform, she got hold of my hand out of that window and drew me as far as the end of the platform. I said, 'Mother, Mother, let me go you'll pull me on the line.' She couldn't let me go. Anyway, I went all the way home crying, down Leys Avenue, 'cos there was no shops hardly on the other side, then, it was still all very poorly. Anyway, everyday Jim used to come home and see me with a crying face, I used to do me work and me cooking. I had never done any cooking in me life. And I was standing and watching and doing things. I never washed a handkerchief until I was married. I used to do it, and me hand used to be raw, when I was washing. Anyway, that went on for about a week, and all of a sudden I thought, well that's not fair to Jim to come home like that and see me, and when I started feeling sorry for myself and

crying, I started singing – on the top of me voice, and the neighbours all knew, 'cos I could sing, I used to sing and the neighbours used to say, 'Oh Maria's thinking about her mother again,' because me mother went home with the two boys. You see me father was buried at Willian, and I was the only girl in the family – she had to leave her only girl behind. I gave up my family, my country, all for an Englishman. And I never regretted it. Never. And that's how I got over it. You see, the people in Letchworth, they were lovely, when I was first here. They were all friendly in the shops. I never wanted to go back and live in Belgium anymore.

There were about 50 or 52 children in my class, so many more because of the refugees. They had to put more desks in the classroom and there was scarcely room to get up between the rows of desks. In one class, Mr Poppy, now he was a very well-known Letchworth teacher – in his class there were 70. Now as you can imagine, he couldn't really teach. Some of them didn't even understand English. A couple of teachers at school taught French, in a rather elementary way. It was quite marvellous. Children adapt.

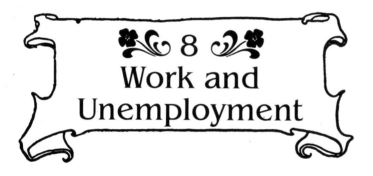

❧ 8 ☙
Work and
Unemployment

The work available for men and women became more and varied as time went on. In the early years labour was needed to build houses and roads, then to put in all the services – gas, electricity, water and sewerage. Very soon others were attracted to the town, businessmen who founded factories that became household names, both locally and further afield. But Letchworth did not escape the effects of the recession of the twenties and thirties and many men for the first time knew what it felt like to be unemployed.

When Mum first came to Letchworth her first job was caretaker of the church rooms – the church rooms in Commerce Avenue – and she kept that job on and became the 'governor' of the church rooms, no doubt about that. Everybody went to her for the bookings, jumble sales, dances, parties, it was quite a lively sort of place. Never got any money, the place hadn't and I am pretty certain, her wages when she first started were about five

Above: *Kryn and Lahy metalworkers casting railway engine wheels.*

Right: *The St Edmundsbury Weaving Works, c1910. The company manufactured many of the banners used by local organisations.*

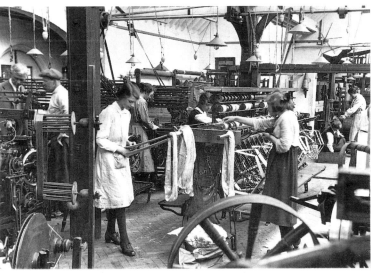

shillings per week, looking after the room, keeping it clean and doing the catering for the Saturday dances and what have you. Then it was upped at some time to ten bob from 1913 until she packed it up when she was in her eighties.

She was well past it in the latter stages, but nobody dared sack her. I went to the local priest, the rector at the time and said, 'Look I am fed up to the teeth. Mum can't do this job, you'll have to tell her to go.' He said, 'I'd rather give up the living than tell her. I daren't tell her!' I will say this, she did chase if things weren't right to her way of thinking, she would have it out with the rector and give him a right going over. It was funny, she was caretaker of the church rooms, she was caretaker of the Midland Bank, and she worked at Nott's all at the same time. She was never at home and was always on the go somewhere. She seemed to just enjoy work; she was not interested in money at all. In point of fact I can remember Dad getting very, very cross with her at one time.

The church hall was a big hall – at least a good 80ft x 30ft – and it wanted a new floor and no way had they got the money to do it. The next thing I remember was Arthur Smith, the local builder, ripping up the floor and starting to put a new floor down. I said, 'Where they found the money from, Arthur?' He says, 'Your Mum.' Mum bought the new floor because it was her room, nobody else's room! Of course, when the evacuees started coming in to Letchworth they opened up a soup kitchen at the church rooms and she was down all the time cooking. I don't know, she was never at home, I'll say that.

My grandfather was Frederick Trask, he came to London from Yeovil to study engineering. When my mother was born he decided to make a pram for her. It was hand-made with a metal frame with metal wheels, but the body was all basket-weave. I remember seeing a photograph of it with my mother sitting in it, and my grandmother pushing it. My grandfather lived in Elmington Terrace in Camberwell in London, and was looking for a nice site to build a factory. Apparently the land in Letchworth was a lot cheaper than in London – and there was also available housing. He took out a patent, it was dated August 28, 1919, but I don't know where the name 'Marmet' originated. He was doing very well; my grandmother was all prepared to move with the children to Letchworth in 1920. My birthday was in the June and he died when my mother was carrying me. She was in Germany at the time with the occupation forces and they sent for her and he died in 1920 in King's College Hospital in London. The factory was all ready to start. He'd come home to organise the move, the family was packed up and waiting to go. He was eating a chicken and must have swallowed a bone and he was in such a state they sent for a doctor. They rushed him to hospital and within 48 hours he was dead. A bone caught in his throat and it choked him. He had a partner but I have no idea of his name. My

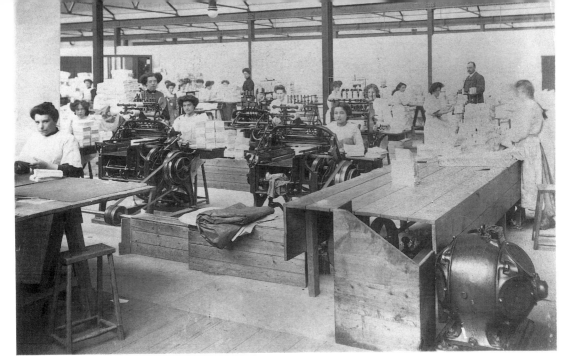

grandfather payed all the money in and everything but he never lived to see the factory working.

J. M. Dent and Sons Ltd, printers, photographed c1910.

The Spirella was a very interesting company, it was American in origin and they instituted a number of things regarding personnel which were hardly heard of in this country in those days. If somebody arrived at work on a bicycle, and a lot of them did, and you had a puncture it was mended in time for you to return home in the evening. They also had capes which you were allowed to borrow if it was raining when you left work at night.

Another enterprising firm were Marmet and it was rather interesting how their name was made up. It was the initials of two brothers – A. R. Morris and E. T. Morris. They were, I understand, a Baptist firm and they had prayers every morning and the idea was that high moral standards should apply to their workers.

My eldest sister who is now 94 used to walk all the way from Arlesey to Dent's in Dunhams Lane to work, and she did that for years. Everyone came to work in Letchworth from all the villages. She said sometimes when she got to work her clothes were wet and they had no facilities to dry them. In those days you just had to do the best you could, and she stayed there until she was married in, I think, 1935. The rest of the family eventually all went to Spirella. It was a great thing to get into Spirella.

I was just a trainee – a tracer on the design of corsets which was great. We went all over the building tracing, working on hospital orders, surgicals and the like.

I worked for Nott's in the packing department and Wegmuller used to be in charge of despatch. When I first went there, there was another Swiss man working there, called Muller, and they used to make their own chocolates. They were very good and at Christmas-time, they made Father Christmases with moulds in chocolate. It was mostly young ladies who worked upstairs on the chocolates. I was trained to make cakes and things. We used to have 12 months with the pastry-cook and 12 months with the cake-hand and 12 months with the sponges. I wasn't involved in bread then, but we used to do all the morning goods – you know the buns, rolls, farthings buns, halfpenny buns. And they'd go round the streets in vans with these things we made. It's marvellous when you think about the cost of stuff. During the winter months when they made a lot of crumpets I had a period with the crumpet man. On a Friday you could start work at six in the morning till nine at night. There was no overtime or anything. All you used to get was a jug of tea and some sandwiches from the restaurant. There were 36 dozen crumpets in a batch, and one batch took an hour and if they made about 36 dozen, well it was only 3d for seven so there were two working all night for less than £3. Well it's marvellous when you think about it. Nott's employed about 14 of us on the confectionary and then they had four bread bakers who worked at night.

They used to do outside catering, too; it's been done on the old Letchworth Recreation Ground there and on the old football field. I remember the Spirella corsetières – well Nott's used to do the catering for them. One of the chaps used to come round preparing their accommodation in Letchworth, but one year I think they had about a hundred – it was in August – and I know that I went there serving at night. They used the garage that was at the back and then they had a huge tent facing. This was to feed all the visiting corsetières. Then they had about five double-decker buses running round for them. They served a whole meal for them. Some used to come every month – about 150 of them – and then they would serve the meal in the Icknield Hall – but this time – I don't know which year it was but there were about 1,000 of them.

You couldn't work at the Spirella until you were 16. I went there in 1932 when I was 16 or 17. When you think of it, Spirella ran a National Health before the National Heath was even thought of. If we had a bad tooth we went to the dentist and they used to pay half of what we used to pay. We used to pay a penny a week into the H.S.A. so they paid half and the Spirella paid the other half so we had about 1/- to pay to have a tooth out.

I was a clerk in the goods office. You stood up at the desk ledges which were at chin level. If you wanted to sit down you had to climb on a stool. There was no carbon copy paper or anything like that. There was a huge press with great big arms on it with balls you turned and a huge book with very thin paper, something like

Steam train standing at the first railway station built in 1905 and replaced by the present station eight years later.

blotting paper, We had to brush the leaves with water with a big whitewash brush. Everything you wrote down had to be written with Indian ink and then you put your sheets of paper between the pages of this book after you'd slopped water all over the pages, and put it in the press, the Indian ink came off onto the sheets of the book and made a copy. When the King was coming through to Newmarket races, they had to warn the crossing at Litlington and there was no phone, so if they wanted to send a message anywhere you had to walk to the signal box and the signalman would punch it out in Morse like the old American businesses, it was really primitive. And just to make sure it was all right they would send me walking down to Litlington to see that they'd opened the gate properly. It's a wonder I never broke an ankle because I used to try to walk all the way on top of the railway lines, balancing.

When I started there I was put on a 12-month contract at 10/- a week. We had to take exams after six months and the results didn't come through for another six months. This was their way of getting cheap labour. I got the sack because I didn't pass and I found out later that only three out of 30 had passed.

It was a good time to start a business although everybody was going bankrupt. We had deflation not inflation, the wholesalers were so eager for trade that I could go into business. I didn't have a shop till some time later. I started with very small beginnings, charging accumulators, selling bits and pieces, and repairing the radios. I went round with the accumulators, and people would say, 'My radio's gone wrong' and if it was a little thing I would probably repair it for nothing. I had a business card made out and I took it to a wholesalers, said I was in the radio trade and paid the wholesale price for the goods. Whatever they were it would be less than all the other shops had paid for their goods, for prices were going down all the time so any shop that had a big stock was at a disadvantage.

I worked as a reader in a publishing firm. It was called The Garden City Press in Pixmore Avenue. I was a good reader. When we got married I had to leave as you were not allowed to work once you got married in those days.

I had a fortnight off from school, I was 14 and I then started work at Chater-Lea's. They used to make bicycle parts and motorbikes. It was just by the iron bridge, at the back of Cook's. I went in there and it was just like going in a coal mine, big old leather belts that turned the machines going right up to a main shaft. I went in there. 'Hello, son,' said Mr Lynch, the foreman, 'what can I do for you?' 'I've come to work here.' 'Oh,' he said, 'we'll put you on a lathe.'

Start off, everything's all right, the lads next to me who were about 16 or 17 said, 'Are you having a cup of tea mate?' I said 'Yes please,' and they said, 'That'll be a penny.' Along come these mugs with tea in them. They're enamel and brown; they look horrible and don't look as if they've had tea in them. My mother had given me golliwog biscuits, a figure of eight covered with coconut. I wiped my hand on the cotton wool. Then the foreman comes along

Ralph Berett, photographed with his delivery vehicle in Bursland in 1932.

and asks, 'What are you doing son?' 'I'm having my playtime.'
'Oh,' he says, 'we work right through our playtime here.'

By W. H. Smiths, there was a little passage and then there was
Moss's. At this passage there was some stairs and that's where I
worked – Porter and Perrin's – they made high class dresses. Very
high class dresses. They supplied Sollershott. They were very
posh people who lived in those flats and when these people came
to the shop they would go to the showroom downstairs where the
dresses were fitted, then when they were finished, the dresses
were placed in a box and I had to walk up to Sollershott Hall
carrying this box, of a fair size, and I got really fed up with that.

I worked there until I was sixteen, then I went to Spirella. My
job was helping make corsets. I was on the machine that did the
eyelet holes down the back. The old fashioned stays. Of course
the Spirella in those days was a very forward-looking factory in
the way it treated its work people. You used to be able to have a
bath once a week – there were about ten bathrooms. That was
quite something, we could all have twenty minutes a special day
each week. And you were supplied with towels and the soap. But
they didn't let you soak for long. We laugh about that sort of
thing now because we can all have baths when we like these days
but then not every house had a bath especially in the villages.

*Workers at the Spirella factory
with what look like bundles of
'stays', pre-First World War.*

Spirella
The Factory of Beauty

I went to the Garden City Press the day after the general strike was called off in May 1926. And I stayed there right up until the war. Of course, the Garden City Press was part of the old 'Cocoa Press', Rowntree's, Cadbury, it was owned by the chocolate manufacturers. They published newspapers mostly – Darlington, York and all the big counties all belonged to the Starmer Group Newspapers. Rowntree's of York used to send a man down with a load of chocolates, a new line, and they would take certain people out of the works and say, 'Now what do you think of this chocolate?' Public relations you see and those of us who were chosen were fortunate, we would have a half a pound slab of chocolate as a reward.

At 21, I went to Spirella and stayed there for 21 years. It was a wonderful and lovely place to work for, and Nurse Webb, of the MacFadyen and Webb place, she was the nurse there and everybody knew she had to look for anything in their heads. If you were ill, you used to have milk drinks for a fortnight. We had health and beauty classes. We used to have black satin trousers and white satin tops, that was lovely.

There was no training given when you left school – you just had to take pot luck to get wherever you could. I went down to the Full Fashioned Hosiery at Baldock where most of the young girls from this area went. It was either that or the Spirella and there again there was no meals although you were there all day. They did have a canteen and I can remember taking, as many others did, a hot meal in an aluminium basin and they used to put it into the oven for us in the canteen and warm it up so we had a hot dinner.

My sister-in-law worked at Irvin's more or less from the outset. Irvin himself used to have a shed where he kept a little plane

Far left: *Spirella dance group.*

Left: *How to model a Spirella corset c1912.*

Bottom left: *The Spirella company made high-quality made-to-measure corsetry and other garments.*

The composing room at the Garden City Press c1925.

The Social Club dance at Irvin's Air Chute factory, held in the works canteen, 1930s.

that he used to fly in. Very often he'd go down on the cart track leading down to Ickleford and he'd take several of the girls who worked for him because it was a very small concern. He used to go up in this little mono-plane and he'd try out his parachutes that the girls had made – he always tested his own goods – and I think it was an American firm that came over here.

I thoroughly enjoyed my years spent at Irvin's and I have been up in his private plane which I found very enjoyable. He really was a wonderful man to work for in every way. The factory and the offices really enjoyed a very good social life. He was good to all of us.

I used to go to Letchworth Golf Club caddying and I could make more money in a weekend than I did in a week at work to start with, I was only around 15 then. They had to pay you. In 1935 it was half-a-crown a round, that was a lot of money in them days and they generally gave you an extra tanner (6d) that made it three bob. You could generally get a round in on Saturday morning, another one Saturday afternoon, Sunday morning, Sunday afternoon and if you were lucky you might get a third round in the evening in the summer so you was getting 12/6d -15 bob and you were only earning ten bob a week.

Factories were built in the '30s with the intention of letting them to firms to start up in the town and to ease the unemployment situation, because there was a lot of unemployment in between the wars. Letchworth perhaps didn't suffer as much as some towns, because of the variety of the work . . . but I can remember the school ma'am coming in and saying, 'Put up your hands whose fathers are out of work.' She was a rather forbidding sort of a woman. But they got some sort of relief I suppose.

The Phoenix Motor Car Company was burnt down and rebuilt and was renamed the Ascot. That didn't last all that time, and the place was ultimately taken over as a training centre for unemployed men. That was the Ascot Training Centre. A lot of fellows came from South Wales, ex-miners. Some of them settled here in Pixmore Avenue. This Ascot Training Centre was a very useful place, they did all sorts of things there. They learnt hairdressing, bricklaying, any building trade, anything like that.

Jobs were quite scarce in 1936. A lot of the girls went to the Spirella in the office. But I didn't fancy that and I applied for a job at the Post Office. I didn't get the first one which was in Letchworth, but they kept me in mind obviously, and offered me one at Baldock not long afterwards. So I started off at Baldock. And rather hated it. It was very strict and then I had the long cycle ride backwards and forwards in the dark. They were open from eight o'clock to half-past seven. Then we had to balance our books after that. So we were at least another hour. And if it didn't

A row of hand-built cars at the Phoenix Motor Company c1912.

The post office staff photo-
graphed in August 1931.

balance we had to stay until it did. It was rather scary cycling home along the cinder path to Letchworth. We had to learn the telephone exchange as well. And I remember one time when something went wrong with the exchange. They kept me on there until ten o'clock. I only did it for a week. And my father enquired, 'Was it right for me to be doing that at the age of 17?' And they stopped. I was relieved as I was there late every night. We had one half day off a fortnight, Thursday. Very fortunately I got transferred to Letchworth in 1939. Otherwise I would have been stuck at Baldock all through the war. Which would have been devastating with that cycle ride. We were still open all those hours at Letchworth but it was so much nicer.

It would be about 1937 I first came to Letchworth. I left school at 14 and my mother brought me to Letchworth to look for a job. I walked down Icknield Way, where the factories are, past the Spirella building, Hand's Trailers and various other factories. When I looked at her she shook her head, eventually we went into Chater-Lea machine shop and my mother was astounded by the noise inside, the chain driven lathes and the things on the factory floor, and I was not allowed to work there. We went across the road to Shelvoke and Drewry, and found out that they wanted a sign writer. So I was sent before the paintshop foreman who asked me to write my name on a piece of paper. So I wrote my name in as nice a round and small hand as I could which he

The Ingrey family of Standalone Farm plus pet peacock.

looked at and studied and said, 'Yes, I think we can use you in our job,' so I was put to the job of signwriter's apprentice, painting dustcarts. I thought that was a contradiction, painting dustcarts, but work was a very high standard, hand-painted signs in a dark maroon, which was flatted down and then gold leaf line transfer put on the front, Roman fret cornice lining at the side and front, then it was varnished, and looking a picture of workmanship it was sent out. It really was wonderful work.

I first went to work at the Fulfa (Full-Fashioned Hosiery Company) which was at Baldock. I know this is getting away

Above: *Workers on the Garden City Estate engaged in the art of building a haystack c1913.*

Right: *Mr South straw-cutting on Lower Wilbury Farm.*

from Letchworth but so many girls worked at Fulfa, which is now, of course, Tesco's, and was Kayser Bondor in between. It had got such a good name because they earned piecework money and when I was seventeen I was earning more money a week than my father. I used to lend my father money and charge him interest on it.

Dad went to work for the First Garden City on the farms. They had eleven farms scattered around Letchworth at that time so there was plenty of work for them. He took care of all the horses. He used to be a horse-bus driver but not a permanent one. Mr Ward was the permanent bus driver with those horses. Dad took over temporary now and again. He also used to take a horse and trap round the estate with the nobs who came to see what was going on in them days. That went on for years. That went on until the First Garden City finished farming. All my spare time when I was about, say, ten to fourteen, I used to spend all my time at the farm with Dad, with the horses which was not far from home in Paddock Close; every summer holiday we were always driving, helping out with the harvest. Other times I would be driving the horse and cart, taking Brussells sprouts to Letchworth goods yard. I felt highly honoured to drive a horse and cart.

We used to have some horses come from London, from the buses, that had got bad feet and we used them on the fields for six months, and then sent them back again. I think that was my best part of life.

9
Getting Around

Bicycles were by far the favourite mode of transport for getting to and from work, although in the early days people had walked considerable distances in all weathers to their place of work. As the century progressed the occasional car made its appearance on the roads, but horses were to be relied on for deliveries for many years to come.

There used to be a horse bus service in Letchworth in the earlier days. It started at Letchworth Corner down Baldock Road, and Norton Way up to the town and then down Station Road and up to Norton and changed round and back again.

The First Garden City Limited had stables. You know the Ambassador Hotel, the building just beyond, they had stables there and the company kept their horses there. They used to take the horses up to Letchworth Corner to change them. Give them a rest and then put another pair of horses on. They had an open wagon. They did have a horse bus, I think it was bought from London and the last time I saw it was when I went to school at Stevenage. I went to the Alleyne's School and I used to cycle from Letchworth and this bus stood up on the fields at the left hand side. I wondered what it was doing there. Just rotting away I suppose.

The first horse-drawn omnibus in Station Place c1911. The service had started in December of the previous year.

Later on a firm called Brome Motors operated through the town, they came from Luton I think. They used to run to Stotfold and Baldock and I can remember during the First War, and even in the Second War some of the buses operated from gas, they had a big sort of balloon on the top instead of the top deck of chairs. Filled with coal gas from the town supply and worked from that, I suppose it was because of the petrol shortage. It was just an amusing thing to see this great billowing bag of gas on the top.

Very few people had private cars. They were for the ultra rich in those days, when an Austin cost about £100 new. We all had cycles. The first bicycle I had to get to Fulfa on, my father must have found in a tip because it had two back wheels on it. The back wheel had a back-pedalling brake so you had just a brake on the front wheel which was very dodgy, and going to Baldock the hill seemed like a mountain. You had to stand on the back-pedalling brake in order to stop, and the times I just missed Bysouth's wall getting round the S bend there because, being young, you were always at the last minute getting to work. But there used to be quite a crowd of us. Then, when we started to earn, we joined a cycling club and I bought a nice racing bike, very exciting and we joined a club and after 60 years I'm still a member of that club – the Nomads. A Hitchin club, but many came from Letchworth and around – we were a huge group.

Everybody had bicycles – well, 99½ per cent had bicycles and at half past twelve the hooters used to go and everybody came out and they were four abreast going one way and four abreast going the other so Works Road was eight abreast in bikes. Hell for leather, but you had to be ultra careful. Don't forget there was still a lot of horse-drawn traffic on the road and it wasn't always very pleasant, it was a bit smelly. And if it was wet roads, you got sprayed with horse manure if you weren't careful. Old Charley Ball still had a lot of horse-drawn carts on the road. Doesn't seem feasible to us nowadays does it? But the roses were good. When the coal merchant or the milk people came along or Redrup and Starking's bread, who had a great big horse in their cart, Mum would say, 'Quick get the bucket, nip out there's a ha'penny for you.' Bucket of manure. Lovely roses.

As far as other transport was concerned if you weren't cycling you went to Hitchin on the bus to do your parading on Saturday night for all the boys, but if you got on at Willian Way it was fourpence return, but if you got on in the town it was sixpence return.

With the open top buses you whipped up the circular stairs to the top deck, and when we got a little bit further through into Walsworth, the conductor would shout upstairs 'heads down' because the railway bridge was low and you could have been decapitated if you weren't behaving yourselves.

This French manufactured bus by De Dion Bouton was seen not only on the streets of Paris but also running a service between Luton and Letchworth. This photo was taken c1913.

I was born in Letchworth in 1911 in Lytton Avenue. Father eventually went to work for John Ray. And when he changed from horse and cart to lorries, the first one was a Vulcan which was a three-way tipper. It sounds good, but the snag was when you tipped it sideways all the ballast went around the wheels. So before you could move off you had to dig it out. So the side tipping was a bit of a pain. It also had solid tyres. I learned to drive on it when I was about 12. I used to practise in the yard and the railway sidings. We had to go to the railway to pick up building material. And the driver used to wedge the lorry by the points and say, 'Now get it out.' So I had to shunt it back and forth to get it out.

Above: *Miss Stabb on her tricycle.*

Right: *Winners of the British Tab interworks 25-mile time trial c1936.*

Below: *Cart belonging to Davies, Ball and Co and decorated for May Day, c1910.*

The Jackman's Place contract was the biggest contract in Letchworth and John Ray got the contract for the whole site. I was still at school then. In those days the lime was bought in Ashwell and it was fetched by horse and cart. Various carts of different sizes in the fleet of vehicles, including a pony and trap for light stuff. Also a steamer – it could carry five tons – it was a Clayton Steamer. It ran for years. But with the advent of motor vehicles it was pushed to one side. It stood in the yard for years, right in the way of everybody. The Clayton was a two-man machine. A driver and a steersman. The driver looked after the speed and the steersman steered the thing. A comical set up really, certainly by today's standards.

The R101 was at Cardington and then the very evening that it set off on its flight, I was up at Hillbrow. This thing came over. It was ominously low then. It came over and of course...it went very, very slowly. It gave me the creeps to look at it. This great thing in the sky. I saw it in flight go over the night before it crashed.

The bus fare to Hitchin was 5 pence return. When I first went to school I went on the train and had a season ticket but when the buses started to get more regular I went by bus. My father agreed that our flower shop could be the depot for the Eastern National Bus Company and they used to leave all the parcels at our shop and in exchange for that we got a free pass between Letchworth and Dunstable. We also had two free passes each year to go anywhere on the Eastern National route. That was our payment,

One of the few cars around Letchworth in the twenties, this one is being driven by E. S. Underwood who, with his brother, owned two ironmongers shops in Leys Avenue.

we didn't get money. We were the only people that had free passes and somebody rumbled it and said it wasn't right to be giving free passes. So they decided to pay us one penny per parcel, but we used to have great big lumps of iron for Kryn and Lahy and Dixons left here, you know, quite heavy things – we didn't have to deliver them – people called in for them. My father said, 'Well I'm not doing that, if you can't give us a free pass I'm giving it all up'. So he gave it up and they started to leave the stuff at the People's House at the top of Station Road. They did it for about a week and it was chaos – People's House chucked the things outside saying, 'We're not having this.' And the bus company came back to us in a week and we kept on with our pass and we were the only people who got a permanent free pass.

We knew the time of day by the horses coming up the road with these tip carts containing sand and gravel. They used to do a lot of work for Kryn and they would come up the road at about 4.30 pm, I can hear Mother saying now, 'The cart's coming up.' We got to know the horses, the men and everything. They used to be sitting on the side. But Grandfather's carts were mostly low ones. He did have the ones where they used to sit on the side, but they were mostly low ones, he used to do a lot of carting for Kryn because there were no lorries. The carts used to be decorated for certain functions in Letchworth, and they'd decorate the horses up as well.

1930s bus in Station Place.

10
Pupils and Teachers

With a few notable exceptions the teachers at the newly-built Garden City schools seemed an amiable lot. Many gave their pupils a desire to learn and put before them ideas and artefacts that fired their imagination and made their time at school a happy one. The choice of learning establishments was wide – parents could send their child to a little 'dame' school with a handful of pupils, a private school, one that taught by the new Montessori method, or to a more orthodox State school where every teacher had an individual approach and the progress of every class was closely linked to the ability and imagination of that teacher.

I went to a small school. Actually my parents belonged to a kind of community, a socialist community in Leeds and they didn't believe in the State at all. I was never sent to a state school. I never really had any proper education. I went to just little schools or somebody taught me. I don't know if mother payed for it, I suppose she must have done. Either that or she did something in return, I don't know. I went first right up to the end of Wilbury Road, not the very end, up the first hill to somebody called Mrs Ironside, she taught her two children, a niece and myself. But I didn't learn much there at all. I was there a year or two. Then I went to a school also in Wilbury Road, nearer to Westholm, it was opposite the Round House. That was Miss Parks there. I don't know how long I was there. Then there was one in Eastholm. Miss Baker and Mrs Clark were the teachers. A lot of the time Miss Baker lived alone and I can remember sleeping there quite a lot. That was probably when I was 13. I left school just before I was 14.

When I was five I started school at what was then the huts in Nevells Road. In those days of course we started school as soon as we reached our fifth birthday, we didn't have to wait until the start of the next term. And so I went to the hut school until the Norton Road School was opened in November 1909 and I stayed there for the rest of my school life. I progressed quite well at school, was quite intelligent, so my teachers always told me, but when I was 13, because it was the First World War and there was a shortage of labour, I left school and started a job at J. M. Dent and Sons.

Right: *The first members of staff at the Elementary School - 'The school in the sheds'. Mr Cyril Pease, the headmaster is seated in the centre of the front row.*

Centre right: *Is this the infamous Miss Vine with smelly pet goat?*

My headmistress was Miss Vine, she was there for years. She had very funny ways. She had a goat. She always brought it into school with her and it used to sit around the stove and it used to burn itself. It smelled horrible. One time she went away on holiday and when she came back she had met this hatter who owned a hat business in the Midlands or the North and they were going to get married. As a wedding present, for the school, he gave us all a hat, the boys had a cap and the girls had 'tammies', Tam o' Shanters. When she married she became Mrs Vine-Smith and that was certainly something different.

My brothers started school at Miss Baker's which was in a house on Eastholm Green, no. 4. There were two classes, one upstairs and one downstairs. They started off there and then when St Christopher's School opened in the Broadway in 1915 they transferred there and were among the first pupils when it opened. There were 13 pupils on the first day.

Staff and pupils of Wilbury Private School c1912.

I went to St Christopher's at the age of nine. It believed in self-government for the children. We were given a lot of tasks to do and a lot of official positions. We were divided into companies and each company elected a councillor who sat on the council meeting where we considered any suggestions or any proposals which were brought up by the school and if we passed any motion it was then put to the School Committee, forwarded to the main school and if it were passed there it became law. The children always took the Chair at the council meetings and at the school meetings.

Pixmore School was a lovely red brick building, but at both sides, one in the boy's playground and one in the girl's playground, was a long bungalow with two classes in each of those. Behind the girls' wooden bungalow was a section of small allotments which two people out of each group would share. So I would share with another girl and that was another of my favourite lessons, I loved gardening. That was Mr Davis that took us for that. He also took us for country dancing. That was something else I liked.

House captains of Pixmore School, 1918.

If it was Tuesday, after we had said prayers in Pixmore, we were lined up in front of Mr Bunn's desk and told to be on our honour to walk to Norton Road where there was cookery and laundry for girls, gardening and woodwork for boys. And, of course, we used to get up to all sorts of naughty tricks on the way up. We used to go through the tunnel where the pigs used to run through from what is now the bowling green through the artificial lake (now the paddling pool), then we would make a detour through the common after spending a ha'penny at Stokes' for some sticky sweets. Of course, after we played games all across the common we were always late for cookery which didn't do us any good in the long run there. Miss Candy was our teacher, very aptly named. She was very tall straight, real spinster lady with a bun. There were pantry monitors and we used to clean the pantry and move all the jars. This happened once a fortnight. We would clear all the jars that would be full or half-full of dried fruit. The boys would be gardening outside and we used to bribe the boys with free handfuls of currants and raisins. Ever so popular.

The Wendy Lodge School was started by a Miss MacFadyen in the house in Field Lane. She was the daughter of Doctor MacFadyen. When she retired, a Miss Jean Frome-Wilkinson appeared. As far as I remember there were only about four

Right: *Pupils of Wendy Lodge School.*

Right: *Weaving looms presented to Westbury School in 1930 by Miss Annie Lawrence of The Cloisters.*

Below: *Norton School gardening class pictured during the First World War.*

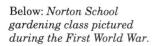

teachers and about 30 pupils. Other teachers came in for a specialist subject. We learnt the usual three 'Rs'. French was quite an adventure, we learnt this by building castles of tables and chairs and books and various other things and learnt the French words as we went along. German was absorbed without us knowing it because we played Bingo, a form of Bingo with picture cards with German words printed on them.

We spent a lot of time outdoors in the garden where we had drill and also country dancing. In school we were taught crafts because we were the children of the Garden City. We learnt clay modelling and the clay was kept in the bath, to keep it moist. And we also learnt embroidery. Other crafts were taught to us at the Cloisters, where Miss Lawrence reigned supreme. Pottery by Deborah Harding, printing by old Mr Blunt, weaving by Miss Lawrence herself. She roped in her odd-job man to show us carpentry, I still have a stool I made at that time, when I was about nine and it's still going strong. And her cook taught us how to make jam tarts. We enjoyed that lesson very much.

Building the new St Christopher's in the Broadway must have been an adventure but obviously some prominent Theosophists were backing it. Chief amongst these was Mrs Annie Besant, who turned up in person at the ceremony at which each pupil laid a brick under the gaze of some bemused looking workmen. Mrs Besant, who was in late middle age, was unusually attired for the early 1920s, having close-cropped hair, a cotton dress, bare legs and white tennis socks and shoes.

D. Allsop photographed at Westbury School in 1931, wearing a prefect's badge, house captain's badge and Herts County medal.

The staff at St Christopher's were easy going and some I remember with affection. Mademoiselle Burton taught French and inspired a love of that language. Mrs Fleming Williams, who composed the school song, taught us music and dancing and was persuasive enough to have 20 or 30 girls of sturdy build, clad in regulation green eurythmic dresses, imagining themselves to be autumn leaves to her piano accompaniment. Her husband, who had been in the RAF during the First World War as an observer, was perhaps less enthused by the ethos of the school than his wife. He taught art and carpentry. I remember when a flying India rubber found its mark and knocked off an intimate part of a male Greek statuette in the art room, he glared at the offender and hissed with passion, 'If you were mine, I would put you over my knee and smack you,' but this kind of retribution was not allowed at St Christopher's.

But of course St Christopher's got bigger and bigger, not with pupils but with people, Theosophists leaving money to build this and build that and build the other. You didn't get the money if you didn't do the building, which is how the theatre became built and the gym and so on. I think there were about 38 classrooms and only about four of them were being used. Which is why they left and went up to Barrington Road and just built two classrooms there, in 1927 I think, something like that.

Once St Christopher's moved to where it is now the school was left empty for a couple of years before the nuns came over. I went round there one day and they said, 'What's this gallery up in this big room?' They thought it was a musician's gallery. I said, 'No, the Montessori* movement started in Letchworth and the training place was St Christopher's and that was the Montessori room and the gallery up above was for visitors to see this new method, to watch all the children.' So they were fascinated to know that I knew about that. Gordon Craig designed the theatre but I thought it was very poor. The acoustics were all wrong.

I went to St Christopher's School when I was about 10 or 11. I don't remember much about the schooling there. Schooling was very easy, if you didn't like it you walked out.

There was a summer pageant. They had a lot of the St Christopher's people in it. It was a mixed school but the girls used to be taught eurythmic dancing. They had these special dresses they wore which were rather nice, sage green, soft material. The style was really loose, but they wore a girdle that crossed round.

In this pageant quite a number of girls took part. Don't ask me what the theme was. I was one of those that Margaret Hunter asked from Norton Road School to be in it. Part of it – I think it was called 'The Seasons' or something – this was the important part: there were four fairly large, big girls, fairly tall, they all had hooded cloaks in different shades – grey, brown, green, I don't know what the other colour was, the Four Seasons, you see. These cloaks had a sort of breast plate, a clasp sort of thing. They were made out of coffee strainers! That's what they used. It was really quite funny.

To indicate the end of an episode of anything two of the girls would come on from one side of the lawn, hands outstretched and the other two from the other side, and they came together and that was like a curtain that indicated the end of that feature.

A year later I went to St. Christopher's School, after spending four years at a very strict boarding school, and I loved it, there was such freedom that I couldn't believe one was allowed out in school hours to go and get an ice cream at Squire's dairy which we did frequently.

In those early days at Norton Road School a new style of education was introduced into, I believe, Class 3A. The class was split into four with what books we had as a library round the four

Rose Turner in a production at St Christopher's Theatre c1914

*(The Montessori method is a way of educating very young children by directing their natural instincts rather than controlling them. Initiated about 1900 by Maria Montessori, the Italian educationalist, who died in 1952.)

corners and they were designated, English, History, Geography and Maths. This was known as the 'Dalton' plan and I believe had been imported from America. You were allowed to sit in any corner and approach any subject until you had completed your syllabus which was set for the week. You could also crib because they believed bravado in some young pupils was essential.

I can remember the headmaster and the teachers at Norton Road School. They were the most hateful teachers if you were poor. We wasn't poor in the sense that we went hungry, or shoeless, or anything like that, but we came from the wrong side of the tracks in Common View. No matter how good you were you were kept down. I was very good at drawing and painting, I think if they'd have taken a little interest in me – my mum and dad had no interest in me – if they had I could have gone a long way. It's in the family because I've got a nephew who is a Master of Arts. If you was poor you were made to feel poor. It was a very hard school, Norton Road. The teachers were no better than evil.

In 1931 the new grammar school was built. There had always been scholarship places to Hitchin Grammar. We were just the age to go to Letchworth if it was open in time. We watched it being built. We hoped it would be open. And then we sat for the scholarship. Most of us at Norton Road sat for it . But there were only 15 places for the whole of the area, which I think included Baldock, Royston, right around. So not many of us got through, of course. I was very fortunate to go to the grammar school, but unfortunate in so far as I lost a lot of friends that way.

I didn't know much about Letchworth when I came but I soon found out. St Christopher's was a vegetarian school and that was something new to me. I used to walk from the station every day, which was about a mile. All right in dry weather but not in the wet. We had to do our walks each morning before breakfast. We were made to walk around the block. There was great emphasis on being out in the fresh air. When we went running we had just our shorts on, nothing else, in all weathers. Classes weren't very warm, especially the wooden huts at the far end. One had a long bar heater. There were wooden sinks in the yard, and we would take our plates, after the meal, and wash them up there. You used to call the members of staff by their Christian names, but the discipline was still good. Some were referred to by their full names, for example Mr Linsay, but Oscar was never known as anything else and there was Humphrey, the maths master.

At Letchworth Grammar School teachers wore black gowns in various stages of decay; the Headmaster sported pin-striped trousers and spats which I took to be part of the academic outfit. He was a Yorkshireman, a pupil of Bradford Grammar; but a period of teaching in an English public school had determined him on a series of outward observances. We had to call the hall, 'Big School'. I was reprimanded for referring to him as, 'Mr Wilkinson'. 'You must not use his personal name; you must say Headmaster.' How was I to know? Some school rules were mysterious: boys and girls were not to travel together. This meant that technically little Geraldine Walker was not to ride home through ten miles of dark country lanes to Sandon with her brother (there was no exception for close relatives). Happily the staff turned a blind eye. The school was not co-educational, but mixed, mostly in favour of the boys. The school hall (sorry 'Big School') doubled as a gym, and there were identical changing rooms labelled, 'Boys' and 'Girls', containing a kind of small swimming pool, or large sink into which muddy boys plunged naked after rugby. Did the architect envisage girls behaving thus after hockey? We just went home in our sweat. Boys studied physics, girls did botany (sex was avoided at all costs, so biology was banned). No Marie Curie or Charles Darwin could ever emerge. It was hard to know how one offended, as good sense did not prevail. I was punished for leaving my seat to sharpen a pencil; this needed permission.

Inevitably, since we were treated as being irresponsible, we behaved accordingly. Within weeks we became young demons; one new teacher lasted only for my first term, and I can remember the door opening, framing the headmaster who bellowed, 'Mr H, a word please,' and poor Mr H went out to be rebuked.

We had a daily morning assembly; the headmaster had one prayer for each weekday, repeated over the years. I am relieved to say that some prayers went unanswered. Every Tuesday, for seven years, I heard him ask God that we might have 'manhood and firm self-control,' but happily there were no sex-changes. He tended to mumble and I pondered on the phrase, 'every assorted evil.' One day, being alone in Big School, I peeped on his prayer desk and found (I might have guessed) 'The Public School Prayer Book.' My intriguing phrase turned out to be 'every assault of evil.'

My mother, busy with her work as joint caretaker of the Settlement, found me a handful. There were no nursery schools, so at three years and eleven months I went as a pupil to the Central Preparatory School in Gernon Walk. It was a small two-teacher private school and it was usually known as 'Miss Holloway's'; she eventually sold it to Miss Lake, who wisely re-named it, 'Gernon Lodge'. Letchworth possessed a number of small private schools; the simplest ones were almost 'dame schools', where a few small children were started off in someone's front room. Miss Bowes kept one in Norton Road, and there was another in Field Lane. 'Miss Holloway's', 'Wendy Lodge' and the 'Madonna' had their own buildings but few teachers, and at Miss Holloway's I worked along happily with older children and made rapid progress.

Above: *Norton Road School Infants 1921-22.*

Right: *Norton Road School's production of Rumpelstiltskin c1939.*

Far Right Top: *Westbury School, early 1930s*

Far Right Bottom: *Westbury School sports day c1935.*

At six years I was in Miss Fairhurst's class, and the good things began. Norton Road was solidly built, with large low windows and a sunny Junior Hall. One day Miss Fairhurst carried in an orange witch-bowl, whose facets caught the light, and she placed it on the black grand piano for us to admire.

I thought it lovely, as I did the flowers and lawns in front of the school. The playground was bordered by large trees, and Mr York the caretaker could climb up them in the autumn and knock down the horse-chestnut conkers for us.

These were the depression years when money for school equipment was scarce. We wrote on small wooden black-boards with stumps of chalk, kept in match-boxes; they were rubbed clean with small squares, which we learned to knit. Each child had a good strong cardboard box for its own possessions; Miss Fairhurst must have had an acquaintance in a hosiery shop, for these boxes had once held a dozen pairs of stockings apiece. They were fascinating, and we improved our reading skills on 'Bear Brand', 'Aristoc' and 'Kayser Bondor'.

Certain days during the year were always anticipated with great excitement. The most important of these was May Day. It has been celebrated on several of the public places in the town, but the schools, too, took it up and none with more vigour and ceremony than Norton Road School.

Preparations began with the election of the May Queen. A blackboard bearing the names of girls in the top classes was taken to each room in turn, and every child over seven had a vote; somehow or other, we all knew who would be elected. Then a practice maypole on a stand appeared in the hall, and certain junior and senior classes began to learn the mysteries of Single Plait, Double Plait, Four Plait, Spider's Web, Gypsy's Tent and The Ring. Four ribbon holders stood with backs to the pole, and the boys advanced to a slow tune to collect the ribbons. Then they turned back and timed their last steps by singing under their breath, 'Give it to your partner and ma-ake a-a bow.' When the dances were over, ribbons were returned, the last bows made and we skipped off in pairs. Some children never did master the intricacies of the plait, and then the ribbons wouldn't unwind, and took a lot of disentangling.

The smallest children learned little invented dances, perhaps rather silly, but I enjoyed pawing the ground as a horse and galloping away to the tune of 'John Peel'. Juniors and seniors did country dances; I loved their tunes and titles, 'Nancy's Fancy', 'Haste to the Wedding', 'Gathering Peasecods', 'We won't go home 'till morning', 'Circassian Circle'. Some senior boys did sword and morris dances.

There was a different theme each year for them: when my little cousin was an attendant the theme was, 'Oranges and

Lemons'. Girls with dark hair and eyes had long orange dresses, and the fair-haired blue eyed ones were in lemon. In my year we dressed as the four seasons; my winter white frock was trimmed with ivy leaves, and I carried holly. Spring girls were in green, summer in blue, and autumn in orange; and once again hair and eyes were matched for each group: the effect was lovely.

We had no amplification in those days, so an orchestra was gathered under Mr Swannell, the conductor, and sat on a platform, specially constructed on the field. Then the Queen's Throne was built, in front the tall hedge. We sat on the steps and ate our cold dinners and talked of glories to come.

For me, May Day was the culmination of the year. It was held on a Saturday and as we hurried along Wilbury and Norton Road we caught up with adults and other children all bound for the field. In a corner by the bicycle shed stood the canopies of the Old and New Queens, with the names painted on them 'Queen Barbara 19—'. Four boys held the corner poles, waiting for the procession to begin.

Spectators sat in a great circle round a grass area planted with tall maypoles, their ribbons bound tightly round the poles. The throne was decorated with flowers and greenery; the whole school was lined up in the playground in processional order, ready to go. The signal was given, the orchestra struck up, and we moved onto the field and into the arena, with little girls in front scattering flowers.

But even this was only a preliminary, there was another pause after we had made the circuit. Then we heard the music for the entry of the Queens, and the canopies advanced, the Old Queen

Although the May Queen was the centre of attraction at May Day celebrations, the boys were also essential to the pageant, becoming attendants for the day, 1909.

Above: *Great care was taken over May Day costumes - for boys as well as girls.*

Below: *May Queen attendants at Norton Road School's May Day, 1935.*

first, in a long white dress and blue train. She wore a small silver crown, the New Queen's train was green, and she was bareheaded. Small pages wearing velvet caps with pheasant feathers carried the trains, and attendants followed. The procession moved to the centre of the circle, where a stool was placed. The attendants withdrew, and a page brought a cushion with the tall crown on it. The New Queen knelt, and was crowned by her predecessor. When she rose, the pages arranged the trains, one over a left arm, the other over a right, and the Queens danced the minuet. They seemed to me stately, graceful, composed, wholly adult, self-possessed. It is strange now to think that one was fourteen, the other fifteen.

The last steps of the dance led to the throne, which the New Queen ascended alone, while her maidens arranged themselves on the steps. She presided over the day, and did not descend till the head-boy fetched her down to join in 'Circassian Circle'.

A little while ago I chanced to read a history of Whitelands College, founded long ago to train women teachers. There I read of May Day ceremonies almost identical to ours. I imagine that some newly-trained teacher, long before I was born, must have started the Norton Road tradition.

Before Norton Road had a school field, my mother remembered seeing a May Day in the Howard Park, now the paddling pool, with the Queen arriving in a pony and trap. One year, when Joan Elcombe was Queen, Letchworth had a Civic Week and we held the May Day in the gardens in front of the grammar school. I did not enjoy it. I longed for the field with the sweeping hawthorn hedges and chestnut trees forming a background for the throne. There the ribbons fluttered, and the bright dresses moved in shifting patterns to the thin sound of the orchestra in the open air before the Queen sitting in glory above her maidens.

*All the children took part in
the May Day celebrations,
whether in fancy dress (left)
maypole dancing (centre) or
as attendants to the May
Queen.*

In 1926 Letchworth had a visit by the then Duke of York who later became King and we had to do our maypole dancing on the Town Square for all the dignitaries. We also had the annual May Day celebrations which were held in Westholm Green and we always had a jester too and he kicked a balloon around which was really a pig's bladder blown up.

11
School's out

Organised treats were a rarity for most children – if they were lucky they might be taken to the cinema or for a Sunday afternoon walk with parents, but by and large they had to amuse themselves. And they were never short of ideas. With a few sandwiches and a bottle of cold tea they would wander over the surrounding fields discovering (and sometimes destroying!) nature along the way. The memories are of a golden childhood where the sun always shone and the summers were long and hot.

I was in the Meccano Group when I was younger. We used to go to the cinemas. There was a cinema where the old Bowling Green was at Howard Park, at the bottom of Leys Avenue, it was called the Rendezvous, that was pulled down in about 1928. It was made completely of wood, if it had caught fire there would have been trouble. I always remember seeing Jackie Coogan in 'The Champ'. After it closed down, they built the Palace Cinema and we used to go there. Old Granny used to live with me, well she practically brought me up, my mother was working in the shop, she looked after me and fed me, and she would take all us kids – about six or seven of us – and she would ask for, 'One eight-penny and eight halves'. If you didn't go with her or any grown-up you had to pay full price.

In our spare time we'd go to the Rendezvous. It was very rough ground then. We used to go to the cinema, our only entertainment. Always Cowboys and Indian films – we clapped when the 'goody' came on and booed when the 'baddy' came on. We stamped our feet, Win's sister went right through the floorboards. The films frightened us – we were not used to films. They were not talking films though.

Then I did Greek Dancing. I do not know how I got there but I thought it was very posh. This was at the Vasanta Hall. We wore

strange looking skirts – tweedy wrap-round skirts and I wore a bandeau on my head. Letchworth was a strange place then. We went to Greek dancing for ages.

We played on the common, we had a free, very nice childhood really. We played without shoes on – went barefoot all the time. When I was at the little school in Eastholm we weren't allowed to go without shoes, so we used to carry our sandals to the gate, put them on, go into school and take them off again when we came out. The paths were paved with tarmacadam, not very hard on the feet. We used to buy shoes and mother wouldn't let us use them all summer.

I recall flying kites and playing marbles. They came round with the time of year, you needed the wind and the weather. I remember having a thick winter coat. I had a kite which I was very proud of and I remember sending it up on the tail of the kite and seeing it from the school window. It must have been some kite to send a coat up. I had seen the kite in the shop and saved up for ages. My grandparents used to send me 2/6d every Christmas and birthday, which was quite a lot in those days. And I had an uncle and aunt who would send me half a crown. I saved them up and bought the kite. It cost 7/6d. It was navy blue. It seemed very big, it must have been up to my shoulder, I must

Norton Common was a favourite place for children to play. This group, photographed in 1928 have made their 'den' there.

have been ten or eleven. And I also sent up a wooden barrel with a metal rim round – I sent that up once on the tail. I flew the kite where the Grange is now, there were fields. We used to play in the fields, there were cows there. And you could walk across the fields at the back of our garden, under the fence, across to Croft Lane and you could walk the other way to Wilbury Road. So we had those fields to play in as well as the common. So it was there we flew the kite.

When the Belgians were here, it used to be daggers drawn with the young ones. We used to get running fights with those. Never any damage done of course. I remember my brother, who was a catapult expert, got really annoyed with this particular bloke. He upped with his catapult and let fly and it hit him on the temple and laid him out stone cold. Of course it got to the police, and I remember a policeman coming down to take him away, and they kept him in the police station all day and issued him with a severe warning. But of course the first thing he did when he came out was to go and buy some more elastic to replace his confiscated catapult.

The artificial lake was dug out in the early days. I think that was one of Ebenezer Howard's ideas originally. It was dug out quite roughly, nothing elaborate at all. It used to be very dirty and unkempt. There used to be a patch of clay. You could almost use it like plasticine. It was beautiful blue clay. Used to make all sorts of things out of it – marbles for one thing. Used to play marbles on the way to school in the road gutters. It was all right then as there was very little traffic about. Where Hilary House now is, is where we lived (in Norton Way). Opposite, the Pix Brook was contained in a concrete culvert. It ran as far as the railway line, and, of course, underneath the railway in concrete pipes. We used to get into this culvert and go down it under the railway and out the other side into Works Road. It was a route to school. Sometimes it was mucky and we'd disturb the occasional rat.

The Heritage Museum was originally the offices of Parker and Unwin. They didn't live there at the time. So the place was deserted at the weekends. We found out at the back, looking towards Rushby Mead, there was three air vents, and just big enough to squeeze through. Once you got inside there was a colossal table and on it was a model of the town, all the houses and streets set out, marvellous model. We didn't do any damage or anything, we just looked around and went out the same way. About six or seven years old.

Howard Park – I remember that before it was built up as it is now, when it was all wooded and with little bridges across and I used to be terrified. I thought that there was awful things in there – daren't go in, across the bridges, very funny really.

There was one amusing incident when I was in the scouts. My friend and I were walking towards the old fire station. And as we were passing, a fireman came out and he said, 'Would you like to help us out?' And being boy scouts what could we say? So we said, 'Yes' and we walked in. He said, 'Come this way.' And he took us out the back and there was this big tower. And he said, 'What I want you to do is go up the tower and I want you to jump out to give our men some practice in catching people in the big sheet.' So my heart fell. So I couldn't do any more, because I'd volunteered and being a scout what else can you do? So I took my hat off, went inside the tower and there was these steps going up and up and up and slowly I climbed up until I got to this window and I climbed onto the window and looked down and I saw these tiny men holding what looked like a handkerchief, and I stood there quaking and the man said, 'Jump then.' So I just closed my eyes and stepped off into space. And I landed in this sheet. And the man said, 'That was excellent.' And my friend got up and he jumped out and he said, 'Very good.' And the crunch was, he said, 'We've got a show on the arena this afternoon. Would you like to help us out by doing it and showing the crowds how it's done?' How could we refuse? Now this is where John Menzies is. That used to be a grass arena. A lot of the Letchworth shows used to be held there. So, come the afternoon we helped the firemen out by jumping out of the tower that had been erected, into the sheets and the crowds were quite pleased. I can't remember what the event was, but it was slightly pre-war and very exciting, but when you're in the scouts you've got to be prepared for all these sorts of things.

Early Garden City fire engine.

Where the paddling pool is today on the Howard Park it used to be just a little overgrown grass pond with plenty of weeds in it. You could take your net and jam-jar down there and you could spend the afternoon having a picnic and catching sticklebacks, newts and tiddlers. Lots of children used to go down there and enjoy themselves. But then it was decided to do away with that and cement it all over and make it, what we thought at the time, a posh paddling pool with stepping stones and the fountain.

As children we used to roam around all over the place. We used to go down Redhoods Way where all the beautiful cherry blossom comes out. On the hill down Bedford Road there used to be a sewage works and there were some smashing willow trees there. We would cut branches and make bows and arrows and play Robin Hood. In this area we used to frequent the Roman camp. It seems funny, it used to take us all day to walk up to the Roman camp. At Easter time we used to make a fire and take a kettle to make a cup of tea. We used to go down to one of the houses further down – I forget the lady's name – but there were only two houses there just beyond the cemetery and the lady would give us

some water and we'd make a fire and have some tea. Of course some time during the afternoon old Mr Brolia – the ice-cream man from Hitchin – would come up. I think they were Italian or of Italian extraction.

In the summer holidays we used to take our tea and go paddling first of all in the river at Ickleford and when we got fed up with that we could come back to sit on the crossing to take train numbers. All the big steam engines would come through carrying out speed trials along there. The Flying Scotsman used to come down about half past five one way or the other so we would sit and wait for that to come down and we would know what the time was. Then there were all the Silver Links, but we were getting a bit too old for trains then. Nothing could surpass the steam trains. Looking back now to some of the lines they pulled out – if they had continued with steam trains they would have been making a fortune now. I have always said if I had the money I would start a grocer's shop and have all the chain money containers – they used to run round the shop to the office and returned with the change. They used to fascinate me. I think they would fascinate all the young kids today. There is no such thing as a tobacconist now – they sell tobacco but not like old Sid Thacker who used to mix it all up for you.

During the time we lived at Norton Way South I remember some huge horses, they raced up the road each evening to get back to their stables near Letchworth House, now the Ambassador Hotel. There was a trough on the green where they could get a drink. We used to wait outside the house for the Wall's ice cream man to come on his bicycle. He came the same time each day loudly ringing his bell. If you wanted him to call, you put a card in your window with a large blue 'W' on it.

Whilst living in High Avenue – they were the days of playing with the top, which you kept going with the aid of a whip and of course the hoop. I remember not holding the stick that batted the hoop tightly enough in my hand and it went straight through one of our windows, and I got into considerable trouble.

One thing they arranged one year, in association with this Boys' Club was a procession and they had this procession in November because it was on Guy Fawkes Night and I remember Bennett's Motors put in this old Ford T Motor Car, which was like a lorry and they had this brazier at the back with firemen all in uniform and they were cooking these chestnuts and throwing them out to the crowds as they went along. The procession then wended its way to the common where we had this lovely big bonfire and fireworks display. There were 'Jumping Jacks' and they used to light them and then they used to jump about two or three yards up high in the air and go off bang with a frightening din. Anyway these hooligans threw these into the crowd and, of course, everybody jumped around and it upset the procession completely.

Far left top: *A delightful picture of young Edwardian girls with their dolls.*

Far left bottom: *The Walker family of Paddock Close c1912.*

Above: *On warm summer days children flocked to the Howard Park paddling pool.*

On top of that they had coloured lights on the entrance to the common and we thought this was great as it was not a normal thing in those days – but of course these hooligans now put them in the dark and broke these lamps. So much hooliganism. It got stopped, I think.

We used to play round Pugh's farm and have our own games of sort of Cowboys and Indians and one we called, 'Stick 'em up.' We used to creep through the barns and have pretend guns and whoever said, 'Stick 'em up!' first won. They were all horses in those days, horses and carts and we used to lead the harvesting tumbrel carts with the extensions on each end with the huge piles of sheaves on top. Half a crown a day we used to get for that, leading the horses back after they'd been filled up by the workmen. Then there was the occasion in Pugh's rickyard when all the ricks were taken apart and the rats were killed. They had the fire brigade up there when they fired the ricks and us boys went killing rats. We used to find nests of them and drop the little pink rats in a bucket of water. Boys used to bring them to school in matchboxes. I should think the rats had more corn than old Pugh. These old stables and barns were semi-derelict with rotten wood, old beams, we used to crawl in the most inaccessible places to hide and we'd get dusty and covered in cobwebs and go home and get a good thrashing for being so filthy.

I remember in Norton Pond there were magnificent newts. Beautiful crested and spotted newts. We used to wipe them out wholesale. I believe there's a shortage of them today. We had never heard of conservation in those days. You just had to tie a piece of cotton round a worm and dangle it in the pond and eventually you'd get one. But you could see clearly in the water because the water was beautiful in those days. Great bullrushes. It always puzzles me why that pond was there. I suppose it was a puddle. There used to be lot of elms in those days, everywhere it was elm trees.

I used to play around Norton Village with Rusty Rogers, he used to be one of my best mates. Always go down the spinney with an airgun, we used to spend lots of time down there, not Radwell, but Nortonbury, and the River Ivel was beautifully clear in those days. He had an old 'Hayden' gun. And the iron bridge across the meadow is still there. I can remember looking at owls' spit balls just by the bridge there. We used to lay under a tree there. One of my favourite pastimes was birds' nesting. My father used to threaten me with all sorts if I went birds nesting. He was absolutely dead against it. I expect he did it. Even in those days he was dead against it you know, if he thought I'd been birds' nesting or had touched any eggs I'd be for it. I never collected eggs, one or two of the lads did but I think they were conscious that there wouldn't be any birds if they collected them all. But hedges were so wonderful in those days. They would be up to ten

Children in Pix Road c1910.

feet high with hawthorn and of course the whole of the Grange, there was nothing there. The first thing you came to if you looked across the fields was this line of pine trees.

I can remember the old days going up to The Cloisters, walking with the whole family, Mum and Dad and five children. No buildings on the Broadway of course, just the old post office there. No library, we used to walk all the way across the fields with the real wild flowers, the cowslips and the poppies and the daisies, a real nature walk and we just loved it, we looked forward to it.

We were never bored in the summer holidays. Played all the usual games, hoops, tops, skipping and marbles, and we were taught to play indoor games as well. We had a very happy childhood, but there was not a lot of money coming in for a big family.

I was in the Girl Guides and had some lovely camping holidays with them and sometimes we just slept in a farmer's shed on straw. Our Guide leader was Miss Mary Ibbetson assisted by Miss Elspeth MacFadyen, niece of the late Dr Macfadyen. On one of our camping holidays I was so hungry after one of our campfire meals that my friend and I pinched some apples from a tree

outside our camp, only to be caught by Miss Ibbetson and Miss MacFadyen. I am afraid that I got into serious trouble as my friend whom I encouraged to pick the apples was my patrol leader and she got into severe trouble.

To earn money we used to meet people with shopping bags and say, 'Carry your shopping home?' and you'd get tuppence or threepence for that. Another way to earn money was to go round with a sugar box and collect horse manure. There were Carter Patterson's horses, baker's horses, milk horses – all sorts in those days and we used to go down Glebe Road, up Works Road, down Icknield Way, up Cromwell Green, Cromwell Road and do our own area. But when we got along Works Road area, that was between us and Pixmore and so my brother or me used to go ahead and if there was a pile in the road we would stand there with the shovel, so if any of them came, we would defend the heap.

The barrow was a Tate and Lyle sugar box on pram wheels. We used to sell a barrowful for 8d, that was a bargain, we walked miles to get it, or 2d a pailful. We used to say, 'Don't run, you'll shake it down.' One person who used to have several buckets was Mr Thomson. I think he used to have several buckets off us every time, so he was all right.

There used to be a fair that came down Icknield Way, on the grounds down there, opposite where Shelvoke used to be. Sometimes there would be a circus and there would be elephants. We would be 'millionaires' at the end of that time.

We used to run a fag card fair. All the cigarettes in those days used to have cigarette cards in and we used to have a fair amongst ourselves down Icknield Way (it's still a field now), down near where ICL used to be, at the top end. We would organise it amongst ourselves. Ball in a basket, ride an old bike – all for cigarette cards.

There was a chalk pit at the top of Icknield Way up Blackhorse Road. It's all filled in now, but it was a big dip. If you look at the beech trees, the branches are fairly near the ground for a beech tree. We used to get an old iron frame, old wheels with no tyres, and go down one side and up the next. It's a wonder we never broke our necks. I'd have died a thousand deaths if I thought my son would do it.

We used to play football. We played at Pond Lane in Baldock. We used to walk all the way, play football and then walk back. We used to go birds' nesting everywhere, as far as Halwell and Weston, all walking.

We'd also play in the road, football, whip and tops, marbles, hoops and skipping. The roads were much quieter, there were only horses. If you saw a policeman coming you'd run off even though you'd done nothing wrong. You didn't want to give him the chance to say, 'What are you doing son?' and get a clip round the ear from his glove for nothing.

Once a year, Monks' were very good, they used to be near the archway in Eastcheap. He used to have Father Christmas come off the train and into a car. He would throw sweets out from the back of the car. It was like the pied piper.

During the school holidays Mum used to want to get rid of us so we'd get packed up most likely with some bread and jam and a bottle of cold tea or something and we'd walk across to Ickleford and paddle in the river and that used to be quite a thing for a lot of the children, either that or the Roman camp. The Roman camp was very, very steep and we used to find old sheets of tin and sit on them and slide down to the bottom.

There used to be quite a lot of children from all round the area paddling in the Ickleford river but at five o'clock, so they said, the sewer was released in from Hitchin. You could always tell, because the water clouded and got thick so you had to get out. Apart from that, the cows used to stand in the water as well, but we never caught anything, we must have been immune. The things you used to do. People would be horrified now.

Letchworth Girl Guides with Capt. Mary Ibbetson c1914.

*Members of 'The Girls' Club'
c1910.*

There were plenty of fields to play in, what we used to enjoy was
going to the river in Radwell, which was three or four feet deep in
parts and swim. There was also a spring of water suitable for
drinking. We also picnicked in Weston Hills. We played games of
marbles, knock-up, hopscotch, skipping and rounders. When the
pavements were icy in winter, there was always a slide outside
the house. Children would play outside in the evening under the
gas lampost until it was time to be called in. We played cards or
dominoes in the evenings, or drawing.

We used to have the Girls' Club, the reading rooms and the
church rooms and we used to have socials there. We had dancing
and whist drives. Hillshott School as it is now, the big building,
that used to be Pixmore Institute was where we used to have
whist drives and dances as well. They used to have concerts there
and my brother-in-law, he won a live pig for singing! I can always
see this little pig – I wasn't very old, only about seven or eight.
He took it to a farmer I think – but I don't remember what he did
with it.

We used to go for picnics – we never thought of keeping in
Letchworth. We used to walk up the Weston Hills to picnic at
Easter time. We used to have relations down from London and
they'd never seen an apple tree – they knew what apples were
but they had never seen them growing.

I played on the green in front of the main gates of the common. Became a member of 'Cook Shaw's Army' after qualifying. To explain 'Cook Shaw's Army', Cook Shaw was Cyril Shaw who worked for Broughton's Pork Butchers, Eastcheap, hence the nickname 'Cook'. At one time he was friendly with one of my sisters whom he used to court with half a dozen sausages.

But coming from a military family Cyril wanted his own little army, I could not tell you how old Cyril was, he was probably fourteen when we were ten or eleven. But Cyril produced a little gang who met on the common and every one of them had to find a straight rose briar in the common, strip it of all its bits and make a bow. Find a straight willow stick and make an arrow and be able to hit a target at a certain distance very accurately. The other qualifications was climbing certain trees in the common, one of which was known as the 'Giraffe's Neck', no branches, you used to have to shin all the way up to get up there. If you qualified you became a member of Cook Shaw's Army that assembled on the green at the bottom of the Quadrant.

In those days one of the things you had to do as part of Cook's Army was to get from Icknield Way to Wilbury Road without being seen by something like four monitors who belonged to his group and if you got from one end to the other you qualified to join the Army.

There used to be the primroses and the wild orchids – everything under the sun – it was beautiful. Then there were the bonfire nights we used to have down Icknield way, near the Idris. We used to sit on guard there all night in case somebody from Pixmore or Westbury came and set light to it before the day. Old

Mildred and Walter Titmus in the garden of their home in Campers Road, 1927.

hot potatoes, stick them in the fire there – black as the ace of spades. Oh dear – oh dear! No butter then – it had to be margarine. We spent weeks building them. Happy days really – although we didn't think so at the time!

In the late summer, when the corn was ripe, a reaper was brought to the field and the corn was cut and bound into sheaves. Sometimes we went on to the field and helped the women stand up the sheaves into groups of four or six called stooks. When no one was left on the field we played amongst the stooks at hide-and-seek or other games. When the sheaves of corn where dry they were carted by horse and cart to the farm about two or three fields away to be threshed by a thresher. Sometimes we got a ride on the cart too. At other times the thresher was brought to the field and the corn was caught in sacks, weighed, fastened and taken away. The straw was built into stacks.

I still remember some very good children's parties run by the Masons in Icknield Hall. They were a real highlight every Christmas. They were fancy dress and the hardest thing was deciding what to wear. One of the great highlights for me was the opening of the Ozone Swimming Pool. It was a wonder to anyone who used it.

There was a lot of controversy about King Edward and Mrs Simpson, the media went to town on it, much the same as they do today. We had a pretty good idea what was going on and there was a typical bit of schoolboy lavatory humour going round. The joke was, 'Why are Mrs Simpson's knickers like the Union Jack?' 'Because they come down at the King's command.'

I can always remember going down to the paddling pool in Norton Way. This was one of our loveliest times. There was a park keeper – it was always kept lovely and clean and spotless. It was one of our high-days to go down there on a Sunday afternoon and have a picnic on the grass with our parents. We would sit and sunbathe and have sandwiches and things.

We used to go to the cinema in Letchworth later. They had the Palace cinema (that's gone now). We used to go there and watch Tarzan and things like that and we'd get some ideas from that and the D'Artagnan sword fight. With Tarzan and his animal tracking, he would dig a hole, and the animal would fall in. Now when we were young, the men used to go to work across these fields at the bottom of Cromwell Road, straight across, where the bridge is now (there wasn't a bridge then), straight to the railway line, through the fence and over the railway line to Ewart's and Meredew's. What we used to do was to dig a hole, about 18in deep, just enough to make them fall over, cover it with twigs and dirt and stuff . . . and then watch. And they used to fall over. Then, when they got used to seeing it, we got a bit cunning. We used to scratch the earth here and then when they went round it, we'd dig it somewhere else, dig it where they were going to walk. The names that we were called. That was one rotten thing we used to get up to.

Another thing, there were wooden coolers, by the side of the railway line in Works Road (where the electricity plant is now), they have them in concrete now, like chimneys. In the old days they were all wood and you used to be able to get under them and provided you watched and didn't get hot water on you, you could catch newts and tiddlers under there. Marmet Prams were new there and we would go and get canes – you know, the sort of beading that used to go round old fashioned prams. They used to throw it out and have a fire going all the time, to burn the scraps. We used to get them and make kites from them.

We used to call the Pixmore boys 'Pixmore Sausages'. I don't know what they called us. The town was divided into areas, you'd got the Westbury area, the Pixmore area and the Norton Road area. I don't suppose the grown ups were like that, it was only us old boys.

We used to go and play with some girls who lived a couple of doors away and I used to come home and say, 'We had some lovely cake, Mum. It was yellow and its got jam and cream in it. It was angel cake. And Mum would say, 'That's the cheapest cake going'. She was a good cook – they couldn't afford much but the cake was lovely. Everything was friendly then, it was more like a large village.

Four 'little ole boys' try to suppress the giggles as they have their photograph taken c1913.

12
Making ends meet

The family relied on the woman to be skilled in many different things. She had to use the often small income to best advantage, providing for everyone but particularly making sure that her husband, the wage earner, was well-fed, and even organising food to be taken to him at work. As a treat mothers gave their children egg sandwiches or tinned fruit for Sunday tea, but jellies and cake were seen only on special occasions. The family had to be clothed and kept in good health, but in the days before the National Health Service doctors and dentists required a fee and as money was scarce, fine judgements were needed as to whether a child was ill enough to warrant spending 2/6d on visiting the doctor and the child had to be almost at death's door before 5/- could be spared for a home visit. But few children seemed to suffer stringent privations – and they eagerly awaited the weekly penny which would present them with difficult choices between the many home-made confections that were for sale.

An unintentional source of entertainment for young and old alike was . . . a fire! The alarm went and all would be on the streets heading for its location. Few were really serious in that lives were not lost, but they presented a talking point for days after and everyone shared an hour or two of real excitement.

My father was a Stotfold man, he was a wirecutter at Spirella in the huts and my mother was one of the great influx of Peterborough people who came to Letchworth. She went to work in the huts and met my father and eventually they got married. The wire that father cut came in from Germany so, of course, when 1914 came the wire dried up and my father got the boot and joined the army in about 1915, I think. Mum went to her mother's in Peterborough for a bit and worked in the flax fields. She became pregnant and I was born in Letchworth. Father came back from the war badly wounded and about 1919/20 he managed to get a job in the Kryn and Lahy, a very heavy, hard, hot job. During that time he worked on the furnaces and they were never allowed to shut down. Consequently my brother and me used to take it in turns to take his dinner to him. In those days we weren't posh, we didn't have lunch we had midday dinner which was a big meal and a big heavy pudding afterwards. One of us kids walked from Pixmore Avenue down to Kryn and Lahy. At the far end of Kryn and Lahy, the furnaces were near the foundry and some days his workmates would say, 'Come on, Wag, let your kids come up.' We would go up this iron ladder among all the sparks until Dad had finished his dinner and we would take the empty dishes home.

It was exciting, but on hot days, especially when we had a dog to take for a run as well, we got back well after half past twelve and we had our dinner and then back to school. For that I think we got about a penny a week pocket money.

My father died and so having two children my mother had to work hard to keep us. She did housework, she used to take washing in and do it at home and go out to people for housework. She did stitching together garments that were knitted by a firm in Letchworth. So she had quite a hard life. I think that she was a very good manager. She must have been. Later, her brother-in-law had a greengrocers' round and we used to have these specked oranges and things. Also we used to have a lot of oranges that she made into marmalade and sold on the round. It all helped.

I wasn't registered as a child, my parents didn't believe in the State, they thought it was a war machine. So I haven't got a birth certificate. Actually my father was sent to prison in Leeds for not registering my brother. I think I slipped in without being noticed. But when my brother was born, father was sent to prison for a fortnight for not registering. I was eating a boiled egg at the time when the police came. It's funny how some things stick in your mind.

I was really cut out for Letchworth because everybody was a freak that came to Letchworth in the early days. We fitted in you see. I'm sure that's why my parents wanted to come. It was a new town and everybody had a garden. A nice place to bring up children. And I suppose by 1913 it was known of, you see. We

Rose and Linda Turner, Rose Cottage, Pixmore Way, 1916.

The Sanderson family, 1916.

Food Reform Restaurant,
'Simple Life' Hotel and Health
Food Store, Leys Avenue.

were vegetarians from the start, I've always been a vegetarian. There was the Health Food Store – they were very helpful with food, they let us have nut butter, things like that. We weren't registered and because my father hadn't registered us, we weren't registered for food either. You had to be registered for butter during the war, but only butter I think. There were shortages of butter, I don't know about meat, because we didn't eat that anyway. But the health food stores were very good, the original one that was before Moss's had it. It was up the top of Leys Avenue and they did look after us. But then butter was not a thing that was vital, was it?

Letchworth had one of the first practices in Britain held by a lady doctor. She had a surgery in her house on the corner of Pixmore Way and Norton Way, next door to what is now the Heritage Museum. Now she nursed a lady who was very ill, a Mrs Cockerell who lived in Pixmore Avenue in the large house near the Garden House Hospice. She had three children and

when she died Mr Cockerell married Marian, the doctor, and he gave his former residence to become the first cottage hospital in Letchworth. Then during the war they decided they would need a bigger hospital. I was at Pixmore School and we used to take money each week. What we called a penny a brick. And that was to be a memorial for those boys in Letchworth who fell in the First World War. I remember Princess Beatrice opening that Hospital. I was disappointed at the time because as I was a child, I was expecting a real princess. Instead she was an elderly lady in a fur coat. That was the start of our Letchworth Hospital.

Food was vastly different then because almost everything was home grown. All vegetables were home grown and we had rabbits and chickens in the garden, fresh eggs. I don't know how my mother did it, but same as all the neighbours of that generation, they just worked, they didn't grumble. They hadn't got a washing machine. They had a scrubbing board and a dollystick and a copper to light every Monday; and it was every Monday rain or shine, ice or snow, and I hated Monday because I knew we were going to get cold beef. I would love it now.

Cold beef with baked potatoes mostly, and pickle or bubble and squeak because there was always a lot of potatoes and cabbage left over. Never a day went by without we had a pudding, either a suet pudding – spotted dick they called it, which was cut in slices and sprinkled liberally with sugar and marge, we didn't often have butter; we had bread pudding, but not very often tinned

Top: *Letchworth Temporary Cottage Hospital (Pixmore Farmhouse) c1915.*

Above: *Nurse M Webb, June 1930.*

Interior shot of Miss Lee's house, Norton Way North.

fruit, that was rather a luxury, a Sunday teatime thing which was lovely. We had good plain honest-to-God food. Yorkshire puddings, that's one of the cheapest puds still made and if the first course was not particularly substantial a large Yorkshire pudding was made, about, 1ft square, and rhubarb or apple cut into it which was liberally sprinkled with sugar. It was delicious. Wouldn't mind a piece now.

I dimly remember the muffin man. That was when we lived at the top of Glebe Road; that would be before I was seven. I believe it was probably a Friday night he would come round. He would come with a tray on his head covered with a white cloth and a bell and would shout, 'Muffins, Muffins' and then there was an elderly lady who would come round with a three-wheeled bike with a barrow in front and she sold sweets. She cycled up from Baldock on that thing.

I used to play football and cricket till I lost me leg. When I was 21. They reckoned it was footballing that caused it. They reckon I got kicked round the ankle somewhere. They took it off eventually, it went wrong – I couldn't walk on it. I was under a Mr Higgs, he used to come from London to Letchworth Hospital about once a month, a specialist he was, orthopaedic man and they had me on the X-ray table. Dr Hector it was, because he used to do most of the X-raying in those days. And they X-rayed it and fiddled about and Mr Higgs said to the nurse something about the syringe. I remember a bloody great syringe with a long needle on it and he started to push it down me big toe, and he looked at me when he started and said, 'Don't you feel it?' And I said, 'Well I can feel you pressing on it.' He said, 'I think you had better go and see Dr Hector on Friday night.' So I went down to see Dr Hector on the Friday night and I always remember it, he said to me, 'Have a cigarette,' which they wouldn't do these days. And he said, 'Here are your X-ray plates, have a look round the foot part.' – and round the ankle was like a mist. He said, 'Mr Higgs will come down on Tuesday and take your leg off.' I said, 'Oh.' He said, 'But you have got to get your parents' consent because you are not 21 until June.' I always remember he laughed 'cos I said, 'It's my bloody leg isn't it?' And that was about it. They as good as admitted they didn't know what it was. I had the operation in Letchworth Hospital by Baldock Road. It was the night that Gene Tunney beat Jack Dempsey for the World Title because they said I was fighting the pair of them when I was coming round. That was the old anaesthetic because Dr Hector came in to me about five o'clock that evening and said, 'Do you mind if we take you straight into the theatre?' I said, 'No I don't mind,' and he said, 'Well, Mr Connolley the porter has fell down the stoke hole and we think he has busted his ribs.' They took me in the theatre and there was Dr Sugget and Dr Watson from Baldock, Dr Ledward, Dr Craggs, Dr Wilson and Dr Hector. Dr

Hector sat at the end of the theatre table He said, 'I'm going to give you the anaesthetic,' and I knew because in those days they put the pad over you and they shook the ether bottle and I always remember it, there was such a clatter and I heard somebody say, 'You'll be cutting somebody's bloody legs off if you are not careful.'

We had a copper in our first house in Westholm Green and it was a great thing in one's life. I mean everything revolved around that, everybody had their hair washed when the copper was on, and the bath, the tin bath was brought out and I'd got this long fair hair which got into an awful tangle and I used to screech when I had my hair washed. I didn't like it at all. Love it now. My father lit the fire under the copper when it was wash day – that was another thing I discovered that people's fathers didn't do, the women usually did that. Then we had a woman come in actually to do the washing. Her name was Mrs Noon. Anybody who's lived a long time in North Avenue would know Mrs Noon.

My father made jam and that's another of my memories, it was this jam-making and the wasps, all the wasps round this jam, it couldn't have been marmalade because an orange was a real treat only at Christmas, an orange in the bottom of your stocking and an apple. Yes, that would have been through the war as well. My father was always Father Christmas and everything was put

Norton Road School Homemakers' Class. Ridge Road, c1910.

into a sack and he used to go out of the back door and we presumably pretended we didn't know he'd gone out of the back door and there was a thump, thump, thump on the front and, 'Here comes Father Christmas. What have we got for you?' And he'd come in with his sack full of things and hand out things as if he wasn't himself. We knew perfectly well who it was but we pretended we didn't, you know, played the game along with him. I think he had his hat pulled right down over his face so that you could only hear his voice. I don't think he dressed up. I can't remember that. I know they built us a doll's house; and how I failed to find it and see it before the day I don't know because I was so inquisitive. It was lovely – it had electric light, it was just simply made out of a margarine box, four rooms and a staircase with a carpet on it which was a piece of braid I suppose and I think our next door neighbour had fixed up a torchlight on a battery to give it a light. We treasured that we did, very much indeed.

We used to have a house garden, but we also had an allotment at the back of our place in Pix Road. It used to be tennis courts in Pix Road but then they let it out as allotments – Mr Gotobed, he used to have it and then he got too old for it and Dad took it on and we bred chickens, rabbits and pigs down there. When it was the armistice of the First World War my father went down to Hitchin and bought three pigs and he was told he would have to get out of the house because you weren't allowed to keep pigs in Letchworth. So he had to get rid of them and they were all slaughtered in that back garden. If you go to Pix Road you'll see the hook on the wall – they hung them over the drain. He got into trouble for it but they couldn't say nothing to him because he'd got rid of them.

Will and Mabel Hardisty admiring a prize rose in the garden of 41 Broughton Hill, c1916.

We had a big long table in our living room and Grandma used to cook this sheep's head. Grandad would sit and pick it clean. He used to say to me, 'What's on there, Roger, is poison.' You couldn't find a bit of meat on there! He'd sit there for an hour picking at this sheep's head. He used to like it for his tea.

We didn't have so much money when I was young, so we were given more filling food. Rabbit, dumplings. Bladder of lard (home dried) was lovely. Had lard on bread or toast. We had far larger joints in those days, and I remember my mother straining off the juices – it was lovely dripping. For Sunday tea there was always tinned peaches and fruit cake. We thought we were rich if we had tinned peaches.

At the bottom of Bursland we had two shops, this is now a self-service store. But there was Waller's and Otway's. Mrs Waller used to make home-made faggots in thick gravy and we used to take our basins down to the shop and these would be filled with these fragrant delicacies. We would spend our weekly penny in

The Brewer children, Ridge Rd.

this shop unless it had gone in Mrs Sly's which was one of the shops on the corner of Green Lane and Norton Road, just a short walk from school in the dinner hour. Mrs Sly used to make vinegar flats. Little pats of dark crisp toffee with a sharp vinegary taste. I can also remember buying tiger nuts – a chewy, nutty confection. At school there was always chocolate bars to buy and to this day I remember longing to taste a walnut whip, but these were far too expensive, a penny Cadbury's milk chocolate would have to do.

In the summer a loudly ringing bicycle bell would herald the 'Stop Me and Buy One', Wall's, blue and white striped ice-cream cart. A favourite from him would be a penny 'Snofrute'.

You could go to a clinic and have your teeth out but in the case of my stepfather he'd already been twice and had either gas or an injection but they couldn't put him out and he had got to have all the lot out so he had to come home. About a fortnight later the doctor and the dentist came to the house and gave him chloroform and took them out. I think that used to be quite the thing to be done then. When you was at school, if you were ill and had to see the doctor you had to pay half-a-crown, about 12½p.

Because if you was ill and you couldn't go out and had the

doctor in, that would be 5/-. And also we used to go to the dentist to have our teeth out and we had to pay sixpence. It wasn't a proper dentist, it was a sort of travelling dentist. I can remember going to the Howard Hall and they just used to have a bowl there and then they'd give you a glass of water to rinse your mouth and spit in, and he just had this chair and he used to pull your teeth out with pincers, he'd just pull your teeth out and they'd all be sitting there waiting.

A doctors's visit was a rare occasion in our household in the early days as there was very little money to pay him and if we could possibly get through the usual childhood complaints unaided we did.

There was a time that will live with me for ever. I had to have some baby teeth removed. This was done at home, on a scrubbed kitchen table. I remember fighting that chloroform mask as it

Wall's ice cream 'Stop me and buy one' in Icknield Way c1930.

was pushed down on my nose. We used to have to go to the dentist's clinic at the Howard Hall if anything needed doing after that. The mothers would sit round the fireplace there discussing horror stories in front of the young patients who were waiting their turns bravely clutching their clean towels to dab the blood and, if my memory serves me right, a sixpence. The school nurse regularly inspected us for nits and there were regular health checks throughout my school life.

My father thought it would be a good job for me to be a dental technician. On one occasion a gentleman came into the surgery, and he had no teeth of his own, so he was what we used to call dentureless, and he had got to have a passport photograph taken to go abroad, and he wanted it done that morning. Well the normal time for making a set of dentures was a minimum of at least two to three weeks. So, we had a box of old dentures in the laboratory, and we sorted out an upper denture and a lower denture, which was nearest in the size and shape as we could get, and we lined them with what was known in those days as composition. It was like a plastic which you heated and it went soft. We put it in his mouth for him to bite on, and it retained the dentures in position. So he shot off and had his passport photograph taken, and he brought the dentures back to us later, and we put them back in the box.

We had one or two quite spectacular fires, Hayes Reynolds, the old rubber company, that went up in smoke and was never rebuilt, and then there was Kenora which was up between the Ascot works and the Laundry. That burned out and was never replaced. And the Phoenix Car Company had a fire and the Ascot developed from there. The Marmet had a big fire in Icknield Way and they had another supplementary works in Works Road, that went up in smoke. The Anglia Match Company used to go up regularly as well, you see outside were these enormous logs which they eventually made into matchsticks.

A great event in Letchworth was when there was a fire. The alarm would sound which was a strident warning like an air raid warning and most people in Letchworth tried to get there before the hooter stopped.

The engine was manned and they came out with a rush and tore off to the fire with us all in pursuit either on foot or on bicycles or by car, however we could get there. And we always made an effort to get there before the flames had been properly dowsed. The captain of the fire brigade was Mr G. T. Hill and he always had his car parked in the open facing the road so that he could rush out of the house, jump in at any time of the day.

The Anglia Match Company used to have numerous fires. Apparently it was caused by the dipping machine and it

The Fire Brigade on parade with helmets, buttons and fire engine gleaming.

happened when they were producing red matches, which I imagine was the most dangerous. Sometimes two matches would be stuck together – they went through the solution and came up and dried. If the drum moved, it was like striking two matches together and then, woof, the whole lot went up. Of course, the fire engine was called out and like most small boys of that time, if we were in the vicinity, we used to chase after the fire engine, not that there was ever anything to see, there were no flames or smoke pouring out, but we used to chase after the fire engine anyway, just in case there was.

In 1937 I went to the grammar school. Occasionally the fire alarm went and the school caretaker, Mr Kitchens, who was a volunteer fireman, would drop everything and rush off to the fire station clutching his uniform to his chest. Everyone would lean out of the windows and cheer. The days of the volunteer fire brigade were quite amusing because one knew a great many of the men involved. Whenever the fire engine went by with them all hanging on the outside, you waved to your uncle or whoever you knew might be there.

Though I was in the fire brigade I spent a lot of time driving the ambulance. I'll tell you a little story about an ambulance experience. The attendant on the ambulance service was a chap named Mayo, Bert Mayo, grand fellow. He was excellent as an attendant, he had done it quite a long time. On this particular day we had to go and pick up an old lady, I won't tell you her name as she has probably got relatives in the town now, but it was in the Sandpits, everybody knows where the Sandpits are at Letchworth – but when we get there there is nobody there. So we open the bottom door – nobody locked their doors in the early days of Letchworth – and I go upstairs with Bert, and there is this old lady. 'Hello young George,' she says. I had known her all my life actually. 'So are you going to take me to the Chalkdale?' The Chalkdale then was the workhouse, you see, well the infirmary actually, the workhouse was attached to the infirmary and it was in Hitchin. So we load this dear old lady up on the ambulance with Bert sitting in the back with her and as we are going down to Hitchin we get to the Union Road, Bert the attendant, through the little communication window between the driver says, 'Drive round the back of the Unicorn.' I says, 'What?' 'Drive round the back of the Unicorn' – that was a pub. So I drives round the back. He says, 'She fancies a Guinness before she goes in.' So lo and behold Bert says, 'I'll have a pint, she wants a Guinness and you can have a shandy, so go and get them. And so I goes and gets the drinks. She sits there and he props her up in the ambulance. 'Lovely it really was!' When she finishes that she says, 'I'd love another one!' So we give her another one. To cut a long story short when we get up to the infirmary, the matron there who was a bit of a martinet, Mrs Knight, she was a lovely old lady really, but she really ruled the roost and when she bent down to have a word she says, 'She's been drinking!' so old Bert says, 'Yes, two Guinnesses of the best!'

When I was at the garage, Masons, we used to supply drive the ambulance if the local chap, Bloom, was out. I was not very old at all, about 16. We went to pick up this old chap from Letchworth to take him to a nursing home in Hitchin. And I knew he was a lovely old chap, he had a big white beard, I remember it now, and he'd got this red blanket. We brought his white beard out over the red blanket and he looked just like Father Christmas, lovely! I knew that there was two nursing homes in the Maples and Benslow. Well Maples is a maternity home, I didn't realise so I took him to the Maples you see, and Bert, stupid like, never said a word, he must have been in a dream. So we go in, open the front door, take him in and I put him down in the hall. First the nurse come and then she calls matron, matron takes one look round and says, 'We'll make the News of the World this week!' So I wonder what she is talking about, then she explained we got the wrong place, the Benslows are up the other way!

13
Relaxation and leisure

Leisure pursuits were frequently energetic ranging from ratting through sport to country and ballroom dancing, and for the less energetic there was always the cinema. Even in the thirties, Letchworth retained its village-like community spirit and had a society or club for almost every talent – choral, instrumental, acting, cycling, swimming and many more – there just wasn't time to be bored. Few people could afford a holiday but most managed at least one 'outing' a year, often a coach or train trip organised by one of the societies. And, of course, not to be forgotten are The Settlement and The Cloisters which, although covered earlier, merit a mention here as being two of the most important social, and educational, centres of early Letchworth.

In Commerce Lane, where the precinct is today, there used to be a large wooden building – it was a snooker hall with 13 or 14 tables – always quite a gathering of players for all the tables were full. At one end of the hall was a counter where you could have tea, coffee, cakes and biscuits and to heat the place there was one of the big cast iron fires which was fed with coke. At the top of Station Road was the People's House, a teashop and restaurant. Next to it, as part of the People's House, was a snooker room (now the Emblem Club) and that was a nice place with half a dozen tables. It was run by Ray Furmston. The People's House was run completely by the Furmston family.

One thing was going out at night with father's motorbike and side car. Up Letchworth Gate on the Great North Road. Park the bike, get out, torches and a dog and sticks. Go around the straw stocks and thrash the rats. I've had rats jump out and run down the side of my coat, I've had rats up me trouser leg. I forget the farmer's name, it may have been Parish's Farm. My father got permission to do this and we went out nearly every night, ratting. Sometimes we'd come back with 20 or 30 rats.

We went everywhere on our bikes in those days – not a great many people had cars – most people did use their bikes. There were very good walks around Letchworth. We used to walk across Pegsdon and we could walk around where the Letchworth Gate is – this was all fields in those days. You could walk across to

The GARDEN CITY PANTOMIME
A DANCE WILL TAKE PLACE AT THE PIXMORE INSTITUTE,
ON FRIDAY, 11TH FEBRUARY, AT 8 P.M.
Songs from the Pantomimes of last year and this year
DURING THE EVENING
Single Tickets, 3/-; Double Tickets, 5/-; Tickets admitting to Balcony only, 1/-.
Tickets can be obtained from members of the Pantomime Company.

The City Dance Band in The People's House, Station Road, 1930s.

Baldock and have tea at the Studio Cafe – which was on the Great North Road and the Copper Kettle in the High Street.

In addition to sport there was a lot of entertainment in the town. We had at one time two cinemas, the Palace and the Rendezvous. The Rendezvous is where the bowling green is in Letchworth. That was the darkest cinema that you've ever been in – it was very popular with the young people! There was also a building, and I can't remember the name of it, on the corner of Lytton Avenue and Gernon Road, facing where the council offices are now, it was a wooden place and we used to have concerts there on a Saturday night and I remember we used to get lemonade crystals at a penny. It was then demolished. There was also the Pixmore Institute. There's a hall there and we used to get refreshments there at the back – a bit like an old time music hall. That was quite a popular place for people to be entertained. The Co-op hall was again a very popular place, there was a Saturday night dance there. Nott's ballroom – on many nights of the week there were dances going on there, and of course it was the Masonic Lodge place as well before they went to The Cloisters.

The Spirella hall also played a big part in local activities. We used to have these 2/6d dances there with one of the best bands in London – a lovely floor. Another very popular floor was the Kryn & Lahy canteen and that was concrete polished like glass.

Top right: *The cast of*
'Floradora' performed by
Letchworth Operatic Society,
1928.

Bottom right: *Mothers and*
babies at Howard Hall, 1920s.

WEDNESDAY, JUNE 5

(Prior to Civic Week)

St. Francis Theatre

at 8 p.m.

❦

CONCERT

❦

An attractive programme will
be rendered by

MISS D. WEST
MISS MILLARD
MR. REG GALPIN
MR. RAY ROGERS

and others

❦

Halfway during the Programme,
the

Public Ballot for
"Miss Letchworth"

will take place

❦

Admission - 1/- and 6d.

Another great meeting place was the Co-op which had dances every Saturday night, so there was always plenty to do in Letchworth in those days.

The Pixmore Institute was like a community centre and it had travelling shows in it all week and most probably a dance on a Saturday. The famous Dan Leno has been on that stage and I have seen him – also Sophie Tucker. It's called the Hillshott Infants' School now.

Letchworth used to have an operatic society and they also had a symphony concert run by Mr Gomersall at the Pixmore Institute. The operatic society staged Gilbert and Sullivan and I was in the choir and we had some notabilities come to take some of the special parts and it used to be staged for a period of a week at St Francis' Theatre in the Broadway. It was very nice. We used to say that Jack Dent had no bones – he could turn himself inside out. He was very, very good. Before then I knew him as the fire engine driver. He was the son of Dent's the printers.

I played piano from when I was five years of age and then I began to play at concerts and I liked accompanying. I learned the violin and played with the Letchworth Brotherhood Orchestra. The highlight for me was when I was about 14, the orchestra was asked to play 'The Messiah', which was a wonderful performance yearly at the Free Church.

Harold Keen was a very well respected musician in the town, he worked at the British Tabulating Company, and he got this choir going for the work people which he put into music festivals that were held at Hertford and he asked me if I would play as an accompanist, I had to work at the Tab, of course.

In Sollershott, the Miss Costellos and Miss May Blossom Li used to have a group of country dancers which I believe is still going – the Staplers. We used to walk up to Sollershot and country dance on the big grass lawn at the front of their house and Wilfred Kitchen used to be there playing his fiddle. That's all the music we had, just the fiddle, and he had a music and piano shop in Leys Avenue. He looked like a musician. He had a shock of hair, you know, the long haired type.

We used to meet at the Co-op en masse, everyone whose parents were members were also members, and you all had a little box given you with a bun and a sandwich and an apple in it and we marched right up to Baldock Road, usually a belting hot day, to the sound of a band, that may have been a Co-op band or the Letchworth Band and you had all the clowns etc, and a show would be put on for you up there on Dunhams Lane rec. We looked forward to it, it was wonderful.

One of the main things that my grandparents used to get me interested in was reading. They started off by getting me to join the library at Boots which is now where the Halifax Building

Society is, and it used to be right at the back and downstairs. After a while I changed over to the Countryside Library which is up where the old Magnet confectioners used to be, at the top of Leys Avenue. And then I used to use the public library which was in Commerce Avenue. So I had a good grounding in reading or was encouraged to do reading by my grandparents and my parents and now we have a marvellous Letchworth library, so Letchworth has been well catered for reading over the years.

About the Hunters. I can remember it must have been before Christmas. We went carol singing or mumming or however you call it. I was about 11, something like that and I can remember Christine Sunderland being with me along with a lot of other children. We used to get roped into these pageants through Margaret Perkins' connection with our school. Alec Hunter was St George and he'd made all the costumes for the whole of this pageant. I think he'd designed them anyway. And he'd got – I think it was really knitted string that had been tinselled or something for his armour. He was very gifted in the art way. He made this dragon. It was probably made of wood or something, but it was very realistic. Well, part of this thing was the slaying of the dragon, but what I can't really make up my mind about is why were the three Kings with their gifts there. One of them was Barry Parker, the architect of Letchworth, and Edmund Hunter, the father of Alec Hunter. He had a weaving business. I can't remember the name of the third one but they all looked absolutely marvellous. They all had beautiful robes. Edmund Hunter was in purple. I believe Barry Parker was in red and the other one was in green, and their crowns were made absolutely beautifully. I mean they were only artificial, but they looked really super. I know we sang 'Here we come a wassailing' and there were other carols.

At the power station I used to work 5½ day week and I started at only 3/6d per week – that's all it was. With Mum being a widow that used to be three bob for her and a tanner for myself. That would be 2d for the cinema, five Woodbines which we used to smoke at the cinema and come out and go and have three penny-worth at Porky Broughtons, whether faggots or pigs' chitlings. Or we had a walk over to Ickleford as they had a dance on at the village hall which used to cost us 2d to go in there. We used to go via the Roman camp. Used to go and get half a beer over the pub – either the George or the one next door to it. That was our night out.

Civic Week in 1926 was quite a big event. I remember a big window dressing competition and my father won 1st prize in the whole of Letchworth for his window. He got £2 for his prize. The Fruit Trade Federation had their own competition for the best Fruit Window in Letchworth but my father wasn't a member so he couldn't enter it and that prize was £5.

In the years between the wars May Day carried on. Then we had Arbor Day – that was organised to plant the trees along the roadsides and the children, they had an Arbor Day from school. Norton Road had an Arbor Day, I think, most years and the avenue of horse chestnuts in the common, I think they were planted on Arbor Day.

Whilst Letchworth even in the early '30s was not considered a village as such, there was a great deal of what you might call village life, in as much as the social life of the town was centred around the different organisations. The church, for example, was a great centre for organisations like dancing, and whist drives, youth clubs, table tennis and things like that, and I belonged to the choir at St Michael's Church in Norton Way South which involved choir practice twice a week, Tuesday and Friday evenings, and then of course on Sunday, the morning Eucharist service, Sunday school in the afternoon, and the Evensong in the evening, so it took quite a bit of time.

In our spare time we'd do country dancing and Swedish drill. Spirella used to organise the Swedish drill. It was a sort of music and movement where we did leg exercises round in a circle. It was a kind of a very light exercise.

The Spirella used to be very well known for looking after it's people. They had quite a good sports club going. It was where the golf course, the pitch and putt now is, up Willian Way. That was the original Spirella sports ground there. There was a golf course and tennis, quite a lot of things going up there.

Our favourite place was up the slanter. It was a tree at Norton Pond, and it's still there 'til this day. All the kids wore the bark off it. We'd play on the tree and get frog spawn out of the pond. We'd go up to Icknield Way and it was called the 'Highway'. Up there

Macintosh Mixed Foursomes Final, August 1933.

Above: *Free Church Tennis Club, May 1934.*

Far right top: *Spirella Ladies' Hockey Team 1920s.*

Far right bottom: *Marmet Sports and Social Club c1930.*

were genuine gypsies. All the tents and things. We'd be there all day. They were such kind, nice people. This was on the school holidays. Not only me, all the kids. We'd also go to Radwell where we learnt to swim. And you had to tread through cow muck to get to the stream. The cows would come and drink while we played in the stream.

At the corner of Lytton Avenue and Gernon Road was a reading room, since demolished, where I remember a slide show of one of the famous Arctic explorers and it was there that Dr Edward gave a talk on his expedition to South America. This was something to do with natural history. He and his wife lived in Norton Road. There was a literary debating society which held monthly meetings in the Brotherhood Hall. Reginald Hine, the Hitchin historian used to open each session with a talk. On Sunday afternoon I went to the Vansanta Hall to attend the Theosophical talks.

There were several sales of work and bazaars held in the Free Church Hall which was of course the first Free Church. My aunt, Stella Dawson, whilst on furlough from the Church from China – she had been sent out there by the London Missionary Society – dressed up in Chinese costume, along with her daughter Ivy and took the Sunday School one day, and did the same thing at Wendy Lodge.

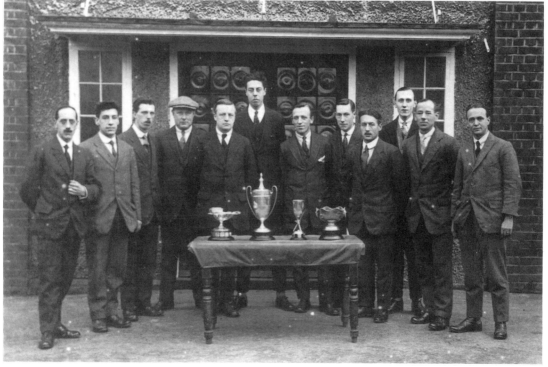

I remember interesting evening meetings at Howgills. Masha Katish gave a talk on how he saw his father sold into slavery in North Africa. He was an enormous African of great stature. Edward Grubb gave talks on poetry and wrote one of our hymns and Mrs Stenna spoke on arts and music. There were many talented families attending meetings at that time. I remember Connor Barrett, who was a sculptor in wood. The family lived at Red Roofs, Icknield Way.

I remember entertaining a party of poor children from London who came to Howgills for the day. They were dressed in thick clothes and not at all suitable for a day in the country, but of course they had never seen the countryside before. This was about 1931. We each had to take two children home for lunch and we had our lunch in the garden. As we were vegetarians they didn't think much of our rissoles, they spat them out over the flower beds. One group was taken to Willian Fields and the other to the common and then they all went back to Howgills for tea. My last memory of the children is watching the train depart and they were leaning out of the window grasping large bunches of grass which they had never seen before and were taking these home instead of flowers.

As one got older, we started to go to the dances locally – there was the Co-op Hall, the Icknield Hall, the Spirella and many other places where you could enjoy yourself at a little dance at a reasonable price. For instance, just before the war you could go to the Spirella for 3/6d – full evening dress for the girls and the men were all dressed to the best of their ability. Halfway through the evening you would go down to the refreshment room for cakes and sandwiches which were all laid out on the tables and there was a very good band – all for 3/6d. It was the same at the Co-op – you could have a smashing time there, but the best place of all was the Icknield Hall. Coming up to the '30s, most of our entertainment in Letchworth in those days was the cinema and the dances, and that was what interested us.

I took French at school – I liked French and I thought I'd like to go on with it so when I left school I went to evening classes at the Settlement. Didn't learn a thing. I played about.

We used to hold the Harvest Home at the Three Horseshoes every harvest time. Grandad used to cook an ox or pig or something, and they used to sit there with their glass of ale and something to eat and sing the harvest hymns. 'We plough the fields and scatter.' That would be in October time, when the harvest was gathered.

Just before the war they had a very good repertory company at St Francis Theatre. I remember that well. They used to put two shows on a week, sometimes they would be playing to about five people. It was heart-breaking. I just don't know how they used to

Norton Village in mid-1920s.

live. I remember some of the names – Paul Courteney, Frank Cavanagh, Effie Bartlett, all of these. One chap – Geoffrey Hibbert – I used to see him on the TV quite a bit in the early days, but I think he is dead now. They were marvellous really what they used to do.

There was a swimming pool in what is now the Ball Memorial Garden. It used to be perhaps 25 yards long. Sunday the water was changed, it was only changed once a week so consequently Monday it was icy cold. But as the week wore on it got warmer and warmer with body heat and all sorts of other things and huge elm trees and ash trees around that shed and everything frll in the water. I believe the man there that looked after it was Mr Brewer and I can see him now walking with his massive great shrimping net getting all the muck off the top. There used to be gents' and boys' swimming, ladies' and girls' swimming and mixed bathing but my father would never allow me to go mixed bathing if he knew I was going. But he didn't always know where I was going. So we had to go to ladies only – very respectable, and it cost us tuppence.

We used to go swimming in the pool at the bottom of Pixmore Avenue, that's where the Howard Gardens is now. We used to have a big shed. The girls went in for one hour or so, and then the men came, and that's how they used to do it. And kids used to make holes, you know, in the wood, they used to pull bits out and peep in at the people getting undressed. I've seen boys do it!

In 1911, the old pool in Pixmore Way was opened and it was a very dirty little pool. It had a lot of little cubicles and it was very difficult to undress privately because either the doors were hanging or some were curtained. It was somewhere nice to go every week and Eddie Robertson, the President, started a swimming club. It started with nine and went up to 93 members. In order that he had a good club he made us come every week and there was a penalty if we didn't appear so it was cheaper to come every week although the water was very cold.

The pool wasn't 100% clean, you can imagine. It was only changed once a week and sometimes you couldn't see the bottom. We always looked forward to this once a week change, although we suffered because the temperature dropped completely and it was icy cold. The temperature was about 46 degrees. Fortunately our swimming lesson didn't start until Thursday so it had a little time to warm up. By Saturday we were enjoying the warm water but you couldn't see the bottom, it was so full of leaves.

In 1935 the Ozone Pool opened and this was a lovely size. It was 165ft by 65ft and the depth was 6ft 6ins to 9ft and they had a diving stage which was up to 16ft 3ins. There was a deeper part where the diving board was.

The Chairman of the Open Space Committee, Mr Fred Nott, declared the pool open on August 2nd 1935 in front of a large crowd of people. There was a tremendous number of children wanting to have their first plunge in the pool and after the speech, on the word 'Go', there was a mad grand plunge and all the children went in. Within minutes the pool was filled. Not only that but Mr Nott decided he would like to take part so he took a plunge himself into the water.

Letchworth Swimming Baths in Pixmore Way, May 1931, where little boys peered in at the changing rooms and knitted bathing costumes were unreliable.

THE SWIMMING POOL, LETCHWORTH.

The first gala that we had after the opening of the pool was the County Championship which was held on August 17 and on that date Miss Lawrence was invited to give the cups and medals.

The very popular 'Ozone' swimming pool on Norton Common, opened in 1935.

Now we didn't go out very often, but one day my grandfather said, 'I'd like to take you all to the cinema.' Now this was the Palace cinema and I think it was about my first time there. We went into the cinema and in those days they had boxes at the back of the cinema and we had this box for our family, and all gas lighting. It was quite good, and made a lasting impression.

In those days we often used to go to the Palace cinema on Saturday afternoon. Mr Percival Westell, who was the curator of the museum later on, used to run a series of Saturday afternoon picture shows on various natural history topics – pictures of flowers and birds and so on and it used to be a special treat for us children to go to the cinema on a Saturday afternoon for one penny to hear Mr Westell give his talk on these various flowers, animals and birds and so on.

For entertainment in Letchworth, there has always been a cinema here, the old Palace cinema which regrettably is no more, because in actual fact, it was the first purpose-built cinema in the country, and I think it was a shame when it was knocked down, but I suppose it was considered unsafe. It was fairly old, the balcony was a bit suspect, and those places have to be up to standard for safety regulations for the public. After the present

*The Palace Cinema,
Eastcheap c1934.*

cinema, the Broadway, was built in 1935, the films was a quite popular pastime. Invariably the cinema was packed on a Saturday night and one had to book if one wanted a seat.

The Broadway cinema was opened and it was very provocative, the smell of the new stairs, rubber stairs. Follow the young usherette, who wore trousers, and had great big torches and pill box hats.

Now one of the big things the church did was to have Sunday School outings. Now our big day out, and we didn't go out that often, was to get a train, and they took us to Hunstanton. Now have you ever tried to control several hundred youths on the way to Hunstanton? And when we got there you had the freedom of the town, there was no control, you just went swimming, or you wandered around and then you met back at some restaurant for a meal. But with our pocket money we used to buy water pistols and on the train on the way back it was a couple of hundred boys with water pistols all firing at one another and I'm afraid the train got saturated by the time we got back to Letchworth. But we used to be tired youths but happy, it was just clean fun and we thoroughly enjoyed it.

The only other place we used to go to was Wickstead Park which was very enjoyable because there's so much to do for children up there. You can go on the lakes, and on the trains, swings and roundabouts and that used to be a happy time. They're about the only two places we went to because holidays were very few and far between. Fathers only used to get a week's holiday and that was unpaid, so they were very careful where they went. I think the only holiday I seem to remember is a week down at Folkestone and that must have been very hard for my father seeing as he didn't get paid for his week's holiday.

My father and mother used to take us for a walk across the fields to the Fox at Willian and on the way over there used to be marvellous wild flowers and silverspoons growing and it was lovely to go and pick them and get to the Fox. My father might have a pint of mild and bitter and I'd have a lemonade and a packet of crisps.

My father was Arthur Cooper Bloomfield and he had a taxicab business and was a coach proprietor. He had a charabanc called the Optimist. There were lots of local outings in the '20s, mostly trips, factory outings and organisations that hired him to go to various places, seaside trips. He did Clacton and places like that. He was always the driver as far as I know. He went up to London and did theatre trips. Then there was the trip to Matlock. In those days, on those hard tyres, which weren't pneumatic, it was tough going, it must have taken ages. They stayed up there in an hotel.

For quite a while there were people around who remembered the Optimist with great affection and when they found out who I was, they used to mention it and say what good times they had in the Optimst. It had a hood, like a pram hood, rather strange, so it wasn't open-topped all the time. But it was such a novelty for everyone then.

Charabanc outing to Matlock in 1925.

The Settlement was built where it is because they thought that the cattle creep was going to be the railway bridge and so that would be in a prime position on the corner – and they blooming well built the railway bridge the other side of it, which put it right in the backwoods. That was the reason for it being built there and of course we practically lived down there, what with meetings and one thing and another.

We used to go to the Cloisters when Miss Lawrence was there with her ear trumpet and they used to have the Letchworth band playing and you'd eye up the girls and that sort of thing. I was 17, I suppose, something like that. She used to always give all the band a present. I know because my brother was in it. They always got a pair of gloves or a scarf, something like that, at Christmas. She built the Cloisters for studying and that, but she didn't mind people coming and in those days you could walk in and walk all round the top. It was quite pleasant.

In 1936 I'd gone down to the Settlement as I wanted to carry on with classes down there – mostly French and English – and I was standing at the counter when I was asked by Ken Spinks if I was interested in the theatre. Of course, I said 'yes' and that's how I got in the Settlement Players' production of the 'Insect Play'. I was an insect running about with a wooden gun! Great fun!

We used to go on a Sunday afternoon to the Cloisters, the men in straw hats. I can remember having to wear a Panama hat and white gloves. Yes, we used to dress up in those days on a Sunday. It was lovely, Letchworth was. We used to walk to where the pond is by the Spirella by the railway, we used to climb over that fence and the field there used to be all lovely totty grass, bee orchids along there, lovely wild flowers. When the Spirella was in full flood before the war the grounds and everything were so lovely. We went through the Dell, used to call it the Dell. You could get to Willian fields from there and come back by the Dell.

14
The churches

Religion played a significant part in the lives of the people – there were apparently 23 varieties to choose from. It was a time when parents insisted their children went to Sunday school and conducted themselves decorously for the rest of the day. Most were happy to do so and some chose the church that suited them best by going to each in turn. As well as providing comfort and spirituality, the churches were also, for many, the focus of social life, organising outings, concerts and bazaars.

In 1907 a group of non-conformists decided there was a need for a church in the Norton area and so they started meeting in a wooden hut on the corner of Cashio Lane and Norton Road. In June 1908, they started a Sunday school, and I went along and I've belonged to that cause ever since – I later became a Methodist local preacher.

In 1914 they built some permanent premises in North Avenue and I was privileged to lay one of the bricks. The Sunday school had announced that if anyone collected half-a-crown they would be allowed to lay one of the bricks on that occasion and I managed to collect half-a-crown.

Then we had an extension in 1924 and in 1934 we built an entirely new church. In those days, of course, there were lots of children in the area. The Sunday school was very progressive. There might be 100 children there on a Sunday afternoon.

For many years my grandfather and his wife had been members of the Salvation Army and they felt rather distressed to come to

Letchworth and find that there was no Movement in the town. They realised that the town was very young and so on. There was, in those days, a very small branch at Baldock and they used to walk along what was known as the 'cinder path' to Baldock to attend services on Sunday. So what they did, being energetic people, was they wrote to headquarters saying that there was this new town called Letchworth and said that they were sure that other people would join us if we established a branch here. So headquarters said that if they found the premises they would send officers. So in 1913 on 26 June the work commenced in the Co-operative Hall which was then on the corner of the Wynd over the Nationwide and the television shop – that used to be the Co-operative store, and the rooms above them were a hall at the Co-op. So they were able to rent that hall for Sundays and during the week they had meetings at each other's houses. That is how it started and officers were sent to Letchworth.

I vaguely remember the origins of the Elim Chapel in Northern Way. It was built by the members of the congregation who became bricklayers, tilers, carpenters and all the rest of it. At one time they held conventions there and a number of people used to come from London. One thing I remember was after one meeting, where people had come in a coach, the coach driver, while the meeting was being held, went off drinking and when the people came to get back on the coach, he was obviously tight – he was staggering about in the middle of the road, his speech was slurred. They called the police and the policeman gave him a good talking to and then let him drive off – can you imagine that happening nowadays?

The instigator of the Elim Chapel was a man called Hubert

Members of the congregation help to build Elim Church.

Stanley Tomkins, drum major, Church Lads Brigade 1925.

Phillips – he was an employee of the Garden City Company. He later went to Africa as a missionary.

For a time I went to Vasanta Hall. I was there for the Theosophists. When I was young I didn't know what it was to be a Theosophist, but by the time I was ten I did. Because I had a cousin born in Letchworth when I was ten, I was quite sure it was my father who had died and come back again. You see, Theosophists believe in reincarnation. I became very, very attached to her.

My parents were Theosophists and they used to go to meetings at the Vasanta Hall which was the headquarters of the Theosophical Society and there was a Sunday school called the Golden Chain which was run on Theosophical lines – I attended for years.

Olivier was the reverend at St Michael's Church at the time and our choir mistress was the wife of Canon Thorndike who was Sybil Thorndike's mother. She was very aged, but very strict. One of Laurence Olivier's sisters was called Sybil after Sybil Thorndike. She was the choir mistress and organist. Many years later my mother told me that they used to have a tea party for the choir boys' mothers at the rectory which was initially in Letchworth Lane and apparently they were entertained with mystery stories. From time to time Laurence Olivier sang in the choir.

As I said we had Olivier here, we had Father Fortescue, David Shepherd, we were really honoured by people who subsequently turned out to be quite important. And of course we had the Theosophists – I don't really know any of them by name but I think they were some of the principal Theosophists of the time.

We also had some more obscure religions here. The Salvation Army were fairly strong here; from the early days they had a

St Michael's Church, Norton Way South, now demolished.

The Free Church with members of the congregation, 1920s.

place in Norton Way. There were the Liberal Catholics and the Plymouth Brethren, and there was a chapel in Broadway which was demolished – it had a front like a Roman amphitheatre.

I was never very good but we went to St Paul's every Sunday for Sunday school. And mostly for evening as well, at six o'clock or whatever. But Sunday school, of course, was nice because we had simple stories and we were dressed in best clothes in those days. The main reason we went to Sunday school was because Dad had a very hard sweaty job during the week and he enjoyed a pint on Sundays and it could have been two pints or even three. After his heavy lunch on Sunday he would get on the settee and have a jolly good sleep.

As a family we went to St Michael's Church – the church was then in Norton Way South. On Sunday as children we went to church three times – morning and afternoon Sunday school and evensong with our parents. This was something we just accepted as our way of life. There were many well-known people at St Michael's, I remember the Mostyn family of Morse Chain. I suppose the person we remember most easily is Father Thatcher. Father Thatcher was such a kindly man. If he saw you out in the street, he would always pat you on the head and say, 'How are you, my little lambs?' We loved it and he was really quite sweet. I remember most vividly in St Michael's – having spoken about Father Thatcher – a lady known as Miss Edwards who used to wear long flower-sprigged dresses and she used to take us for Sunday school. Miss Edwards to me was a great character – we were in awe of Miss Edwards – but she was delightful company on Sunday school outings. For Sunday school outings we were taken to Hunstanton – that was just about the favourite venue for our outings.

St Nicholas Church Sunday School c1922.

In particular I remember Good Friday – that meant getting up and being at the Old Hut in Spring Road (then called St Gabriel's) and being there for a service prior to being in church, where we stopped until after the crucifixion time at 3 o'clock. Then we went back to St Gabriel's where we made things like crosses and anything to do with Easter, then back in the evening for a lantern lecture – things in fact which we thoroughly enjoyed, and we also took for granted as being part of our lifestyle. We did not protest very much – even if we did it would not have made any difference – as far as my mother was concerned, 'That is what you are doing and no use making any fuss about it'.

My brother and I used to go to St Michael's for Sunday school. We didn't stay. We'd go in and get our attendance star and then nip out and go to The Cloisters to hear the bands. Somebody who knew us saw us one Sunday and told my father. He followed us and sat at the paddling pool. We went in, got our star and came out. 'Back,' he said, 'and come straight home afterwards'. My father insisted we go to Sunday school. When we got home we had to stay in. We weren't allowed out to play.

I remember the Reverend John H. Bailey, he was a very devout man. In Passion Week, Holy Week before Easter he used to go round preaching in the streets and of course he had no amplifier or any of those things, but he had a terrifically powerful voice. Very nice. He used to say, 'This is your vicar, the vicar of Norton' and people would come out and stand in their doors because he had no competition from radio or television. They used to stand and listen to him. I went out many times when he did his preaching. And on Good Friday we had a procession of witness from St. George's Hall, Norton Church Hall – up to the old church – where we had the service and of course at Rogation time he would go along Icknield Way to bless the factories and he would give a special blessing to the British Tabulating Machine Company because they were very generous towards Norton. Originally there were three bells at Norton. There are now eight bells and the British Tabulating Machine Company paid for one.

There was a tennis court near the Three Horseshoes and I can tell you something about that. Of course John H. Bailey was a great Sabbatarian and when they installed the bowling green, they didn't play bowls on Sunday. And then Old Man Ireland of the Three Horseshoes and the People's Refreshment House Association started up with a couple of tennis courts at the back of the bowling green. Well, of course, that narked John H. Bailey so he wrote to the press about this desecration of Sunday. Anyway he could do nothing about it and had quite a war with Ireland about this. You see Ireland was governed by the Refreshment House Association, so on Sundays before we started

Bowls Club, Three Horseshoes Norton, First World War.

Right: Many diverse beliefs were catered for, and 'The Citizen' in 1934 carried announcements for many of them.

the service we all had to file out there at the end of the west of the church, across the road was the tennis courts and we sang a hymn so lustily that the people playing on the tennis courts could hear that the church was still functioning.

I remember Laurence Olivier being a shepherd boy at the nativity play in St George's Church and we knew them quite well, although we were potentially Quakers. Basically I was a Quaker, but practically I've tried them all. Funnily enough the only one I didn't try was the Roman Catholic and then my mother and my sister both turned Roman Catholic, my mother because she like drama and she found the Quakers rather tame. She liked the splendid colours and so on.

We went to the Free Church – the young people and the music attracted my sister and I. They had a jolly good choir which they augmented for their big oratorios and things like that. It was quite something and every Good Friday they did 'The Messiah' and they did a couple of other concerts during the year. 'Elijah' was a popular one. I was in the choir. You had to have an audition – there was a terrific waiting list.

Letchworth in those days was very religious and I remember there were probably about 23 different churches and many denominations. It's always been in my mind that somebody wanted shooting when they built the college at Letchworth after the war, that they pulled down the beautiful facade that was of the then-called Primitive Methodist Church. I suppose it went into disrepair at the back because during the war it was used as an ambulance station, but the facia was good.

Letchworth in those days on a Sunday was quite a quiet place. One could almost say 'dead'. People went to church and not only was there plenty of churches but also different religions met in various halls. I went to the Grammar School at Letchworth, I remember that some pals and myself decided we would spend Sundays going to different churches to find out what they were all about and one thing that always intrigued us in those days was spiritualism – it all sounded very eerie to me – and we went to a meeting of spiritualists and a clairvoyant came down to the Settlement. So apart from the churches in Letchworth there were various halls that held these particular meetings. I think the spiritualists held theirs, one of them, in the Settlement, as I said, and another above a shop in the First Church of Boston, Massachusetts, the Vasanta Hall.

15
The developing town

In the early years the layout of the town was set, some shops were built along with many dwellings to house the growing numbers who wanted to be a part of this new venture. By the twenties the skeleton of the town was there, fleshed out as more businesses opened and yet more people came to work in the growing numbers of factories and shops. And it is at this point that this volume of Letchworth Recollections *comes to an end – the town is still developing, but some families have been here for almost a generation. These, then, are just a few memories from that period.*

I joined the Citizen as a junior reporter but left after a short period to go to Southend on a newspaper there. I rejoined the firm in the mid '30s and one of my memories of that time was of a young man coming into the office and saying to me, 'Publish this.' He handed me a letter without the slightest smile on his face and no 'please' or 'thank you.' I remember him clearly because he was so extremely curt. About two or three weeks later I was looking out of the office window; I saw a hearse driving by with a policeman sitting by the coffin and on enquiries I found that the body was the young man who had been so rude to me earlier on. It turned out that he had had an affair with the wife of a local man and when the husband confronted him about it, in a lane off Wilbury Road, he sneered at him, which I can imagine was quite effective and the upshot was that the husband shot him about eight times. This meant reloading his revolver, because his revolver had only five shots in it, so it was quite a deliberate murder.

I went to the trial of the husband at Hertford and he was defended by Sir Norman Burkitt who made a remarkable speech in defence of the husband. I remember he used the phrase, 'sunk in the sea of sorrows.' The upshot was that the husband was found not guilty of murder but guilty of manslaughter and was sent to prison for three or five years, I can't remember which.

There used to be a Boys' Club near where the Broadway Hotel is and to help with funds a fête was arranged on the Baldock Cricket Ground. One of the organisers came round and asked my father whether he would donate a piglet for the 'Bowling for the

Co-operative Society Stores and van, Eastcheap, late 1930s.

pig' stand. So my brother and I helped my father to catch this piglet from the sty and load it in this wooden crate. We put it on a milk float which we used to take round. We had the big milk churn in it and took it to Baldock Road Ground. You can imagine our surprise when we dismounted to find the crate was empty! We then had to retrace our route till we got to the crossroads near the Willian turn, where we heard screams and screeches from the front gardens there and it was after much garden disturbance that we were able to recapture it and apologise for the inconvenience caused. I can assure you that catching a small pig is a lot harder than it seems! They are very, very wily.

I remember when the new council offices were opened which are at the end of the Broadway and I can roughly remember going round this before it was officially opened because it opened to the public so they could go around and see what the offices of the town were like.

In Commerce Lane (now part of the shopping precinct) was a blacksmith and I spent many happy hours watching horses being reshod. Next door to the blacksmith was a low wooden building which was used as a billiard hall. This closed when Burton's shop was built in Leys Avenue and the billiard hall was placed above the shop and is still there today.

Further along Commerce Lane was another wooden hut known

as the Animal Centre. One of the mainstays of this was a lady called Mrs Cotton whose husband, and later on her son, were Letchworth firemen and they lived in what was known as the firemen's cottages in Commerce Avenue. I remember it used to cost you 6d to have your cat or dog treated (that's if you could afford it).

One of the most dangerous crossroads in Letchworth was at the junction of Pixmore Way with Norton Way. And shortly after someone was killed on the crossroads it was decided to erect a red flashing warning light in the form of a lantern strung up on a cable between two steel posts over the crossing. This light used to be confusing to strangers to the town and it was not unusual to see vehicles stopped at the junction waiting for the light to turn to green, which of course it never did.

There were quite a few vegetarians when I first came to Letchworth in 1932. They walked about in sandals without socks and open-necked shirts. It was quite the thing in those days. I can remember when I first went to St Christopher's I was surprised when some of the masters taught in open-necked shirts and shorts and sandals. People like Reg Snell and Oscar Bachaus. Lovely people they really were. All the staff there were terrific. I suppose that's why I stayed so long.

We went to see the train go by carrying George V to his funeral. We had to stand off the bridge because you mustn't be over the King. There were fields all along and I can remember going out of the office and going to watch the train – the train with his body on. It was a purple colour, the coach, and everybody stood all along the railway with their hats off. There were a lot of people standing beside the railway to watch it go by, all the way along.

When I first started working at Boots the takings for the whole week were just over £100 – £102 or something like that. My wages were half-a-crown a week. I was an apprentice, you see, on a three-and-a-half year apprenticeship. Of course everything was sold loose in those days. Lots of loose things in the drawers: there were senna pods and they used to sell white lead, you name it we sold it, unbelievable. I think it was on my first day I broke a large bottle of orange and quinine wine which was a tonic in those days. You could buy thyroid tablets over the counter quarter, half, one, two, three and five gram tablets. All kinds of things you couldn't possibly buy these days.

Top right: *Station Rd 1930s*.

Bottom right: *Leys Avenue 1930s*.

I was apprenticed at Booth's in Baldock, 5/- a week, and they had a shop in Leys Avenue called the Bon Marché and I used to be sent there to help during holidays and always on a Saturday. For lunch I used to go to Moss's and get two slices of ham for 6d, two crusty rolls from Nott's, two bananas from a fruit shop in Leys Avenue, for a sweet course, and then to Squire's Dairy where I got a little pot of cream and two ounces of butter and then I

LEYS AVENUE, LETCHWORTH

The Arcade c1928.

returned to the shop and that was my Saturday lunch, year in and year out. And I went there for quite a time. It was the days of commercial espionage. Hundreds of garments were marked at 1/11¾d, well, I used to have to go to Spink's, and Nicholl's and look all around their windows to see what merchandise they were selling the same as ours. If theirs was 1/11½d I had to come back and knock all those farthings off our price tags. That was done time after time, after time. It was a nightmare to me adding up all those 1/11¾d.

There was a lovely china shop on the other corner from Pugh's, starting from Eastcheap, Miss Clark and Miss Linnel used to run it. It used to stagger me, I was earning £1 7s 6d per week and they could come in there and buy three pairs of shoes at three guineas a time. I wouldn't believe they could spend that amount of money when I compared it to what I was earning. However that was my wage and I was quite content with it at that time. I used to travel on the train with another Baldock girl. I had a season ticket for the train which cost me 12/6d a month to get me backwards and forwards.

Then I went to work for Lilian Reed and once she knew I had

done Pugh's windows I had to do hers. She was a bit of a tarter. She'd have you outside. And all the other shops used to laugh, you know. She says, 'You've got room for a pair of gloves there, and you've got room for something else there.' I thought it spoilt my windows, but you'd got to do as you were told. We had to pull the heavy sun blinds out. And after Miss Reed had burglars we had to carry a big heavy wrought iron gate from the back and put it up and padlock it. So you couldn't get through to the front door. Previous to that we had to bring the cycle rack in as well, that was heavy. The arcade was lovely before the war. It was a very nice place, it really was. There was Cliff with his cycle shop on the bottom, then a health food shop, a hairdressers, Lilian Reed's, Miller with his cakes – used to make lovely cakes. Richardson vegetables. Then I think Brooker's took over a shop. On the other side was Tilley's, a fashion shop.

You were always called 'Miss'. They never had Christian names like they do now. And, of course, a cup of tea or biscuit was upstairs out of sight. No sitting on a stool with a Nescafé mug like they do today. It was a very, very strict routine in those days. Of course it was very long hours for very little money. Anyhow we survived. Then I used to save 2d or 3d a week out of the half crown I used to have pocket money. When you'd got 6d you went to the Post Office and bought a stamp – National Savings stamp, and put it on a card. That was my first attempt at saving.

When I was about eight or nine there were a lot of gypsies in Letchworth. I can recall how they would come round with an old can and my mother would fill it with tea for, say, some pegs – because they used to make them themselves. Or you would give them some rags and they would give you pegs back. They used to

Civic Week 1935.

camp up near the top of Wilbury Hills where the Roman camp used to be – actually in the spinney on the left-hand side of Wilbury Hotel or they would camp on the old Icknield track going down to Ickleford. They used to camp a lot down there because there was an actual track and they could take their caravans down without getting bogged down as it was quite solid ground and they could drive the horses up and down. Then in those days half-way down that track there used to be an old Italian tramp – his nickname was John-John – and he lived in a tin shed and we used to go and talk to him and he would get some potatoes from the local fields and he would bake them and talk to us over the fire and perhaps give us one. He was always digging. He grew carrots and a few odds and ends. Not much vegetables because up there the chalk was only a foot down.

The nearest shop, where we used to go to do mother's shopping, was down the bottom of Bursland – on the corner. It was called Mrs Waller's and next to it there was a shop called Otway's. Mrs Waller's shop was also the Post Office, run by her, and then on the left of the Post Office would be the grocery and greengrocery. On the right-hand side would be the sweets and tobacconists. Her husband was never actually seen in the shop. He was a man who did the errands. If they had orders he would always deliver all of them. He never drove – he was always on his trade bike with a basket on the front and you would see him going round all the houses. He was a miserable old devil, but that was beside the point, she was always very, very good to us boys, especially for myself because we come from a large family. If you went in for a half-penny bar of chocolate or a farthing sherbert she would say if you can't pay today you can pay next week – as a joke – but she was a very generous lady. Everybody went to Mrs Waller's because she was such a nice old lady to us children.

There were eight children in my family but it wasn't the biggest family in Abbott's Road. That was the Barnetts at the other end of Abbott's Road – they lived at no. 4 and I think they had a family of 14 all told.

In them days it was very nice to go across to Willian fields – those fields were all open. It was the nicest place to go blackberrying as young children and also getting the cowslips. It was very nice – we used to spend many an hour walking across those fields. There used to be all the big bullocks in them days – because that land was owned by the big farm near Willian Pond called Parrish's Farm. The other two farms in Willian near Letchworth were Norman's Farm and Tucker's Farm – they are under the Corporation now.

I know in my days on the ambulance, you see, we were out with the ambulance quite a bit, much more than you were with fires and you got to know everybody in the town. Everybody knew you – it was great really and it was a time of great friendship, you

The Broadway Cinema which opened in 1936, almost next door to the Palace Cinema.

know. It was a wonderful town Letchworth at that time, it was so friendly and you walked down the town and you spoke to everybody because you knew everybody. It was fantastic. I can remember, where the Midland Bank is now, on the pavement leading out to the road there used to be a horse trough there, there was a bus stop once. A horse trough supplied by the Friends of the Animals or something like that and my brother and I always used to bathe in it. Yes we did! And I can remember on two occasions George Brown, who was the Clerk of the Council, getting hold of us and saying, 'This is enough of this, and taking us home.

I joined the Operatic Society who were about to start rehearsing for 'Merrie England' so that they could present it during Civic Week. Civic Week was held in Whit-week in June 1935 and most of the town was involved. It was held in the aid of the hospital – which was at that time self-supporting – and all sorts of organisations and individuals were involved in Civic Week in one way or another. The Operatic Society had only seven weeks to rehearse the whole of 'Merrie England' and that included Easter weekend, but we did it. It was held at St Francis Theatre and we had a thoroughly good time. The only night that we didn't perform was on the Wednesday night of that week – when they had a wrestling evening.

The new Urban District Council Offices, built in 1935.

I can remember the electric light coming to the houses, because we had gas in the houses when I first came to Letchworth, and I can remember them changing over to electricity and the magic of the first time switching a switch down and the light coming on in the room, without having to light the gas mantle!

I think one of the greatest memories I have of those days was the contrast between the pavements and the roads, the asphalt in London and of course there were tarmacadam roads in Letchworth and paths, with a lot of grass, the greens, the various greens in the roads, it was part of the construction. The houses were built behind the green, which gave a great impression of airiness, and open spaces.

I was 14 years old when I first cycled here, and being amongst all the cyclists, it looked a busy sort of a place to come to. And all the work that was going on, every factory down Icknield Way seemed to be busy doing something. Hand's Trailers were turning out stuff, the Irvin Air Chute factory were turning out work. Spirella, Marmet in their locations, they were turning out work. It really was a busy place. Walking around town, in the lunch-break sometimes, you saw various people that would make you sort of raise an eye, people in Indian dresses, one or two chaps I'd seen in shorts, riding queer bikes, and of course characters of some note I suppose, but peculiar to me in those days, I must say! Dance halls – the Icknield Hall, the Co-op Hall, all the various amateur dramatic societies there seemed to be in Letchworth doing their little bit, putting plays on here and plays on there, and Scottish Societies and Irish Societies. There was a sort of an arrangement of people and things to do. It was a very lively place.

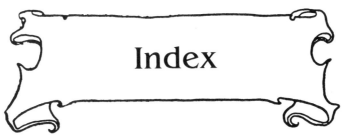

Index